WILLPOWER

WILLPOWER

FINDING THE STRENGTH

Lisa Stephens

New York London Toronto Sydney Tokyo Singapore

Grateful acknowledgment is made for permission to use excerpt from "I Whistle a Happy Tune" appearing on page 73:

PRENTICE HALL PRESS
15 Columbus Circle
New York, NY 10023

Library of Congress Cataloging-in-Publication Data

Stephens, Lisa.
Willpower: finding the strength/Lisa Stephens.
p. cm.
Includes index.
ISBN 0-13-960675-0
1. Will. I. Title.
BF611.S73 1991
153.8′5—dc20 90-48360 CIP

Designed by Rhea Braunstein

Manufactured in the United States of America

10 9 8 7 6 5 4 3 2 1

First Edition

To

Yogi Amrit Desai

The silence from which all knowledge flows

and

W. J. I.

More than words can say

ACKNOWLEDGMENTS

This is really Yogi Amrit Desai's book. Though he played no role in the book's creation or writing, he is the source and the inspiration for the concepts contained here; he has patiently taught me and guided me for the past fifteen years; his work and his life have molded my definitions of excellence and dedication. Any errors and incomplete understandings are, of course, my own.

This book also belongs to the brothers and sisters of Kripalu Center for Yoga and Health in Lenox, Massachusetts, and particularly my colleagues in Toronto. Each and every one of you will never suspect the profound influence you have had in the creation of this work.

Lesley Dove Holmes—with her husband, Donald—has been the still, quiet flame. Many times has she sat in meditation in my stead and carried this book in her heart.

Marilyn Abraham of Prentice Hall Press has been my Maxwell Perkins; and Sheila Curry, her able and subtle alter ego. Every writer should be so fortunate.

Steven Axelrod believed in this book long before it was written, and his professionalism and dedication helped make it happen.

Sheila Baker, Steven Baker, Nancy Damitz, Peggy Metzler Immen, Phillip Unrau, and Dr. Michael Sirisko each provided invaluable commentary on the manuscript.

And none of this would exist without the love and support of my beloved husband, who's been there all along.

CONTENTS

INDEX TO INNER WILLPOWER EXPERIENCES

FOREWORD

There is no one in the world who can do for you what you can do for yourself. No matter how much you receive from others—no matter what you achieve in the world outside you—there is nothing so dependable as your own inner source of fulfillment.

This book can help you discover that source and learn how to sustain a lasting connection with it. Gently and gradually, Lisa Stevens leads you on your personal journey inside the peace and power that lie dormant there.

Often we begin such journeys only to encounter evidence of our negative traits and weaknesses and to abandon the journey in the quicksand of denial and self-rejection. This book shows how to avoid that trap, through accepting the negative rather than denying it, and through reinforcing the positive strengths that are available to us once we learn how to access them.

Lisa Stevens has a talent for presenting profound teachings through everyday events and experiences. The techniques she offers unite the practical with the spiritual. Spirituality, in this context, has nothing to do with religious ideas; it simply means being in touch with the vital consciousness that is the essence of life, the consciousness from which permanent personal transformation arises.

Willpower: Finding the Strength will help you access that consciousness—the strength, power, and wisdom that lie hidden within you.

YOGI AMRIT DESAI

Come, sit down beside me.
Let yourself be comfortable.
This is not really a book.
It is an experience
to be entered
to be enjoyed
to be used
for your health
your life
your joy, and your
experience.

1

Willpower Is the Path, Not the Goal

Most people think of willpower as the magic—and missing—ingredient in their lives. Like the keys to a Ferrari, willpower gleams silently, just out of reach: the mysterious key to changing your life, to losing those five—or more—pounds, to getting into shape, to quitting smoking, to starting—or completing—that project. Willpower can seem to dangle elusively, just out of your grasp. "If only I had *it*, I'd automatically be skinny, healthy, cigarette-free, and successful," we think.

Willpower may work wonders, but it isn't anything automatic or instant. It isn't a "thing" at all. Achieving improvement in your life is actually a constant, ongoing process.

It isn't something that happens all at once, but little by little, day by day. It's something that happens time after time, a succession of small things that add up to a great thing. It's a constant process of trial and error, of growth, and of evolution.

It's little steps, one after the other, that will carry you on the longest journey, that will see your greatest dreams come true.

The secrets of building real willpower are hidden in this process of traveling, in the way you go about reaching your destination, and not in the destination itself. Destinations and goals are useful only in that they provide you with a direction for your journey; they don't automatically provide the means to get you there.

Willpower Is a Process

Willpower is all about the process: the How—the means—of your travels, and not the Where. Willpower is actually a set of skills: skills you will acquire as you follow through this book, setting into motion for yourself the process that can eventually carry you wherever you'd like to go.

What, really, is willpower? Willpower is the ability to act consciously in the present. This means that with true inner willpower, you are able to do what you choose to do, as you need to do it, with full awareness and commitment. You are acting from choice, from personal freedom, and not from compulsion.

Inner willpower is user-friendly. Willpower works with you, not against you, or in spite of you. True willpower isn't some elusive force that you use against yourself to bludgeon yourself into submission.

True inner willpower does not "make" you do something in spite of yourself, your desires, or your intentions. It will not take you where you do not want to go. Inner willpower is a natural process of gathering and integrating your energies right from the center of your being outward. It is the integration of your mental, physical, emotional, and spiritual resources into a body-centered awareness that *allows* you to act effectively in the here and now.

Inner willpower teaches you that there's never any point in saying to yourself: "I'm going to force myself to do this." Because you can't sustain that kind of force. You've divided yourself against yourself, and the action inevitably collapses from the strain. Using force may work once or twice, but it isn't willpower. You'd become your own victim, hurt and afraid of your own cruelty to yourself. You can't live your life that way. And you can't grow strong and secure that way.

WILLPOWER IS INTEGRATION

In this book, you'll learn to work with yourself, discovering and harnessing lost or wasted energies, integrating them into your life as you go. You'll discover that you do indeed have the wherewithal to act as you choose.

You only need to learn how to contact your inner willpower for it to become available to you. Yes, willpower is waiting within you to be tapped. But in the stresses and distractions of your everyday life, perhaps you've lost your way and forgotten where—and how—to get in touch with it. You may not even believe that you have any willpower. But you do. And this book will show you how to find and nurture it.

This book will take you step by step through the process of tapping and using your inner willpower. The book is arranged as a set of carefully programmed and balanced exercises designed to bring you the true experience of inner willpower. These Inner Willpower Experiences are carefully designed to give you the specific skills you'll need to tap into your inner willpower easily and naturally on a daily basis.

This true experience of inner willpower may not be what you expect it to be at all. As my friend Mark said after completing the Inner Willpower Experiences: "It's no wonder I never thought I had any willpower. I was looking for it in all the wrong places! Everything about this technique is much simpler and gentler than I'd expected. And much more effective."

There are four key skills to inner willpower, and you'll be learning them as you go through the Inner Willpower Experiences. They are:

1. Awareness
2. Self-acceptance
3. Conscious action
4. Creative affirmation

You don't need to burden yourself right now with complicated definitions; we'll discuss each of these skills in detail as you go through the book. Each of these skills is, however, used in something called the present moment—which you are about to experience in the next chapter—and each is important and useful on its own. But when you put all four together, they create the conditions that allow your inner strength to function naturally and freely.

The four skills of inner willpower will grow with practice. They will become more familiar and strong and useful the more you use them. This book can introduce you to the basic experiences, and always be available as a refresher, but it cannot turn these experiences into useful skills unless you choose to practice them often enough to make them your own. It is up to you to take the Inner Willpower Experiences in this book and make them uniquely your own.

Willpower Bonuses

Along the way toward mastering these inner willpower skills, you'll also learn how to make your body a powerful tool of your inner willpower, how to clarify and use your inner priorities and motives, and how to use your everyday activities to strengthen and enhance your willpower.

You'll learn how to drop unwanted habits and create useful new ones. You'll uncover the secrets of "won't power." You'll learn how to apply your inner willpower skills to your diet, exercise program, getting things done, overindulgences, and other areas of your life that you'd like to improve. You'll even learn how to gain the upper hand over binging.

And beyond that, inner willpower can teach you about self-confidence and inner strength, about harmony, balance, and inner security. And perhaps—even a little—about happiness itself.

2
The Key to Inner Willpower

The easiest way to begin learning about inner willpower is not by discussing its theory, but by getting some practical experience.

Learning about inner willpower is a lot like learning about kissing: you'll know much more about it if you try it yourself than if you just read about it. It's much easier and faster to grasp crucial inner willpower skills simply by trying them out as you read here, instead of by plowing through a lot of words without any real experience of what it is that you're reading about.

And, like kissing, it's easiest to get the most out of the Inner Willpower Experiences that are woven throughout this book if you begin each one without too many preconceived ideas about what you'll get out of it. It's much more fun to try each Inner Willpower Experience and enjoy it for what it is than to worry about whether you're doing it "right."

Like falling in love or tasting chocolate for the first time, it's real experience that actually teaches you. Just reading doesn't tell you much about some things if you've never been there yourself. Once you've had the experience, words on the subject can open themselves to you with a whole new meaning and power. I want you to taste inner willpower, not just read about it.

Begin With Experience

This book is really about experience: your experience.

This book is meant to be experienced and used, not simply read or skimmed. It is arranged so your inner willpower will develop naturally as you read if you try out each Inner Willpower Experience as you go. As you continue to practice them, you'll find that the strength of your inner willpower will begin to develop naturally and productively.

You've got to do the Inner Willpower Experiences as you go through the book, not just read through them for "later." Simply follow along, allow yourself to float easily wherever the book takes you and try the ideas on for size as you go. You'll find them interesting, comfortable, and useful.

If you aren't ready to experiment with an experience now, put aside this book and come back when you are ready, or you'll be wasting your time and cheating yourself. Just as no amount of reading about how to improve your backhand will ever substitute for picking up that tennis racket and taking a few trial swings, you can't learn anything real about willpower just by reading. You'll be left sitting at the door without the key.

Adjusting Your Headset

First, you need to adjust your headset—the space between your ears. In order to get the most out of this book, your receptivity should be such that you can learn by allowing some space between these words you're reading—space for the ideas to slip through to your inner being. This is a learning process that can't be rushed.

After all, the point of reading this is not to finish this book—

or even this chapter. The point is to learn some real willpower skills that can help you along from here on.

A great deal of your actual ability to absorb and own the inner concepts presented here depends on the physical state of relaxation of your body at the time that you are learning. The more relaxed you are, the more deeply and effectively the learning can penetrate your whole being.

Tension and distraction create physical as well as mental blocks to a complete understanding of the principles being presented here. Whenever information is input into your body, your particular emotional and physical circumstances at that moment are stored in memory also. That means that you can most easily retrieve and use that knowledge by returning to the same physical and emotional state.

That's why, when you've learned to do something while you were tense or excited or afraid or in love the information may seem fuzzy at other times but returns quite easily as soon as you find yourself—and your body—in the same circumstances. It is imperative for learning the skills of inner willpower successfully that you gain this knowledge in its most potent and useful form—via a relaxed, neutral, comfortable body. That way the skills can sink deeply and easily into your whole being, and can be retrieved with minimum effort.

Introducing the Present Moment

The key to unlocking the skills of inner willpower is learning to shift your focus from one of reaching your destination to the process of traveling itself.

Shifting your focus of awareness into the present moment is a specific skill, a knack that can be acquired, like learning to ride a bicycle or steer a car. It's actually something you do quite naturally throughout the day without thinking about it. But to unlock your true inner willpower, you'll need to learn how to consciously shift your focus. Then you'll have the key to open the four basic inner willpower skills: awareness, self-acceptance, conscious action, and creative affirmation.

To begin learning about the present moment, be sure that you are sitting and reading this in a comfortable place—somewhere quiet and secure where you can read and think without distractions, perhaps in your home, office, a familiar corner of your favorite haunt, or in a park or garden. If you are presently sitting in a crowded airport or plane, I suggest you put this book aside for the time being, and pull out a favorite novel instead. It will be easier for you to learn this technique if you are in a less hectic environment. If you've just finished eating, wait at least an hour after your meal to begin. You'll get much better results.

Inner Willpower Experience No. 1: The Present Moment Exercise

Settle in, take your time. Sit comfortably; make any adjustments to your posture or to the room that will make you more comfortable.

Sit quietly; allow those sounds and activities which are happening at some distance away from wherever you are sitting to continue without you, as though you were invisible to them. Let them be. Unplug yourself from them.

Now take a moment to look around the place where you are sitting. Go ahead: stop reading this and have a leisurely look. It's important.

Notice the ground or floor. Really look at it: notice, for a moment, how solidly and quietly the floor supports everything, how securely and patiently it waits. Take your time; notice the floor. It has nowhere to go, nothing to do, but be here with you.

* * *

Notice the other objects around you. Go ahead: have a look.

See how quietly they rest in their places, how comfortably, how silently. Notice that there's no tension, no wasted energy in their position. They simply are wherever they are, comfortable and quiet.

Begin to feel some of the comfortable stillness of these familiar objects. Notice that they seem to create a quiet, protected, perfectly still zone surrounding you and extending beyond your body a comfortable distance. You are sitting at the center of a quiet, peaceful place. If anyone or anything enters this quiet zone, observe how they do not affect it but merely pass through it.

Now take a deep, slow breath. Heave a deep sigh—let it go; let any sounds come out; no one will notice or care. Take another deep breath. Take a few more; you've needed this all day.

Now relax, and breathe naturally, without changing anything.

Keep breathing comfortably, but when you breathe out, allow yourself to let go of all of the events and tensions of the day, as though they were leaving your body along with the stale air. Let them go. Let it drop. Breathe out all those minor tensions. All the frustrations. All the activity. That's it: let them escape from your body and dissolve into the sky, far away from you. Let go.

Notice that every outward breath is continuously expelling old, stale stuff that no longer has anything to do with you. Let it go. Relax. Stop "working"; let the breath come naturally.

Keep breathing naturally and letting go with each outward breath. Take your time.

* * *

Feel how your body has changed slightly from when you began this experience, how it's become somehow different. How? Perhaps it's feeling a bit lighter, or freer. Maybe it feels heavier and more solid. Just notice; that's all. There's no "right" way to feel. You don't have to change anything.

Perhaps there are some emotions flowing out of you along with the outward breath. Fatigue? Relief? Boredom? Stress? That's okay: just observe them and let them go, along with everything else, flowing away from you, old emotions that have nothing more to do with you. Let them go.

Notice now that, somehow, you are breathing in more deeply, too. Feel each inward breath. Experience it.

Observe how each inward breath is completely new and fresh for you. Notice how different each inward breath feels from the outward breath. Feel its newness, its energy.

Breathing normally and without changing your breathing, take a moment to compare the inward and outward breath. Feel how this inward breath changes you. How it lifts and brightens and refreshes you. How each one brings you new energy, new life.

Take your time; this experience is an important part of your learning.

You may want to close your eyes for a few moments. Go ahead. Come back when you're ready.

Breathe normally. Relax. Is your breath coming more slowly and easily than before you began? Is it deeper, or more shallow? Are there any natural pauses between the breaths? Notice any differences. You don't have to do anything; just notice your breathing.

* * *

When you're ready to continue, quietly gaze again around the room, without moving your body or changing your breathing any more than necessary. Notice how the familiar objects and surfaces around you seem somehow different—perhaps clearer and brighter to the eye—how each detail of the room seems more apparent. Has the room changed—or do you have more awareness now? Are you simply seeing more clearly than before? What's changed?

You may even feel that the air between and around each object and surface seems to be somehow changed. Is it lighter? Heavier? Quieter? Brighter or darker?

Simply notice the room; there aren't any correct answers, only the reality of your experience right now. There isn't anything that you're expected to do, or see, or feel. Just breathe. Just be conscious of being here in the present moment. It's that simple.

Welcome to the Present Moment

This is the present moment: the eternal, continuous now. This is the now that expands infinitely in all directions as your awareness of its presence expands. This is the now where time has no meaning, the true reality, the pure consciousness.

This is the present moment in which your life is truly being lived. Welcome home.

How does your body feel? Do you feel any different than you felt a few minutes ago? Simply notice how you feel; there's no need to change anything. Savor this moment; it's a valuable learning tool.

If you've skimmed over this section, wanting to get to the "good stuff," go back to the top and begin again. This *is* the good stuff, but you'll never know it unless you do it. (If you're convinced that nothing about your body or inner state has changed at all, even subtly, you might want to go back to the beginning of this chapter and read it again slowly, following along with your actions.)

Congratulations! You've just learned—and experienced—a very critical inner willpower skill: how to use your ordinary breathing to shift your mental and physical focus, at will, into the present moment. You've slipped easily and naturally into the here and now, simply by focusing on your breathing, and dropping everything that's not a part of this present moment. You see how quickly and subtly it changes your awareness?

But I haven't done anything, you may say; I've just been sitting here breathing—maybe I've missed something? No, you haven't missed anything. Your present experience is really all that you need to have right now.

Experience is reality. Learning to trust and appreciate your own experience is a vital part of finding your inner strength. So don't worry if this exercise seems awkward or silly at first. Try it again tomorrow. And don't worry if your best friend raves about how wonderful the experience was, yet you thought it was dumb. The truth is, your "dumb" experience is every bit as valid and important as someone else's "marvelous" one. And you should never be willing to trade your experience for somebody else's opinion.

Whatever it is, it is. Your experience isn't necessarily anything dramatic; all that you need to understand is that by using this simple breathing technique, your body feels somehow different than when you began. Perhaps you've become more comfortable or quieter. Perhaps you've become aware of an old ache or some lingering tension. That's okay too. It's real progress.

What's important is that you noticed exactly what you experienced and how you felt within a specific set of actions that you initiated and controlled. This is the very, very bare bones of beginning to understand and assert your conscious control over your actions and yourself. Trust in yourself is the foundation of your inner strength. Your experience matters, whatever that experience may be.

What the Present Moment Exercise Does for You

There's a very basic willpower truth hidden in the Present Moment Exercise: when you start focusing on how you are now instead of how you just were, or how you think you ought to be, you'll feel better instantly, and more in control. Simply by breathing consciously, you've brought all your mental and physical energy easily and naturally right here, into one place. And that makes everything else you'll need to do or learn infinitely easier.

Take a look at where you are now: sitting here and reading this book in a relaxed, comfortable frame of mind, thanks to a simple breathing exercise.

This is actually a very important accomplishment: you've experienced your first practical demonstration of your own inner willpower. You've chosen to use your body's natural abilities to gather all your scattered energies together, to drop outside influences, and to bring yourself into the present moment. You've corralled a lot of parts of yourself that have probably been running wild during the day; you've gathered your whole self together into one place at one time.

Everything else that you will learn or experience with this book will flow from your use of the Present Moment Exercise. This simple exercise is the key to the basic inner willpower skill: that of being fully here in the present moment. It's important that you take the time to learn this basic skill well. It's best to repeat the Present Moment Exercise at least once a day for the next few days, perhaps each time you begin reading another section of this book. It's the fastest way to make real progress.

Inner Willpower Is a Way of Being

You may be feeling a boost of personal energy after you've done the Present Moment Exercise. Simply by being "all here now" you've eliminated a lot of scattered energy wasters: energy spent worrying about the future—even the next ten minutes—or regretting the past—even that last petty annoyance that you probably clung to as you sat down here. Funny, how quickly they'll slip away when you allow yourself to let go of them, isn't it? If your mind wants to follow those thoughts, bring it gently back to this room, and this page. Let the other thoughts be. We've more important things to work on here, in this quiet space you've created for yourself.

Why is learning this process of entering the present moment so crucial to understanding inner willpower?

Because willpower is a *process,* a way that you *are* that allows you to do what you really want to do.

Inner willpower is also a way of being, a state of inner centeredness from which you can act with real freedom, confidence, and commitment. It is contained in the physical state of being "all here now" in the present moment—relaxed, comfortable, secure, aware of yourself and your environment. The Present Moment Exercise teaches you how to enter this state easily and naturally.

Some Different Strokes

In the Appendix, you can explore some interesting variations of the Present Moment Exercise that use sight, sound, and physical sensation as different points of entry into the present moment.

Since different people have different preferences in these areas, try each of them as an experiment; you may find that one of them "clicks" quite naturally with your personal taste and temperament. Then you can easily practice it whenever you want to collect your energies into the present moment for better willpower.

It is very important to master entering the present moment. You may want to speed ahead through this book, but don't shortchange yourself by skipping this key exercise. Take the key with you. You'll obtain much stronger, more effective results in developing your willpower.

Now that you've found this key to inner willpower, you can easily learn how to use the first major skill that you've unlocked: your awareness.

3
Increasing Your Awareness

Entering the present moment is the key that unlocks your inner willpower because it brings greater awareness. And awareness is the first major skill of your inner willpower.

Awareness will ultimately give you everything you need to really gain control of both your external situation and your internal resources.

You may think that you haven't got very many internal resources, but it doesn't matter. Awareness will put you in touch with those parts of yourself that are secure and confident and focused, parts of yourself that you may not be conscious of. Once you begin to connect comfortably with these aspects of yourself, your inner willpower can start to grow naturally because you've connected with the place where it comes from.

Being Where Your Body Is

Awareness is the ability to live fully in the present moment. Awareness means being "all here right now," bringing all of your energies together into one place. Very simply, it means being where your body is. No more, no less. Simply being where your body is right now, sitting here in this room.

Awareness is focused purely on sensory input; on seeing, hearing, tasting, feeling, and experiencing everything just as it is, right now. That's all.

Awareness doesn't make evaluations or judgments. Awareness is not the constant commentary of your mind: those nagging comparisons, droning evaluations, lectures and sermons to ourselves that we all know and love. Awareness is pure input, just as it happens. It is about collecting the maximum data, right here, so that better, more informed evaluation can come later.

Expanding Your Perception

Awareness also enhances your perception. Think back for a moment to an especially pleasant vacation you've had, and recall the setting. See the view as you remember it. Sense the temperature, the time of day, the sounds and activities. Take a moment to remember.

Each day seemed filled with so many things, didn't it? But how long were you actually there? A few days? A week? Two? It probably seems like much longer in your mind's eye, and everything about it still has a glorious intensity.

That's not simply because you were on vacation and your surroundings were different. It's because you had dropped your habitual perceptions and were naturally practicing awareness in that beautiful setting. Everything was new, so you entered naturally and fully into the experience of the present moment, and spontaneously became absorbed in precisely whatever you were doing right then, without thinking about where you'd just been, or worrying where you would go next, or any of the usual distractions your mind poses for you. Whatever you had in front of you was all that mattered.

Even today, long after the vacation ended, it remains with you much more vividly than whatever you did this morning. That's your awareness at work. And you can apply that natural skill any time you choose. Because awareness functions purely in the present moment without past memories or fears for the future, it brings freshness to whatever you're doing.

Living with Awareness

Awareness is wherever you are.

Suppose you've turned on your exercise videotape and begun moving to the music. Awareness notices the stiffness in your muscles, the color of the carpet, the arrangement of the room, the gentle warmth of your blood as it begins to circulate, the stretch in your upper arms as you reach forward, the release of tension in your shoulders as you let go. Awareness feels you breathing, feels the fatigue and exhilaration as you move, feels the air on your arms as you swing through it. Awareness focuses purely on where your body is right now. It has nothing else to be or to do, but move with you through the motions of your exercise video.

On some days, awareness watches quietly as you walk past the VCR, pick up the exercise tape, and put it down again. Awareness feels the guilty stab, the frustration and sense of incompleteness. It just observes, without commenting. Awareness walks with you to the fridge, observes as you open the door to see if anything has changed in the last five minutes, as you glance again at the exercise tape, and as you suddenly remember a "very important" phone call that you've been meaning to make for the last three days.

Awareness sits down with you, picks up the receiver, feels the texture of the chair against your back and the buzz of the dial tone in your ear, and spends twenty minutes chatting. Awareness, again, is simply where your body is. No more, no less.

Which is not to say that if you're practicing awareness as you walk or eat that the little voice in your head will suddenly turn off. As long as those little neurons are sparking away, they'll have something to say—mostly old, outdated opinions repeated for the umpteenth time. But you don't have to listen. You don't have to pay attention to that little voice. All you need to do is focus on where you are, where your body is, and what you are experiencing right now.

Living in the Present

We actually spend most of our time, and our awareness, being mentally and emotionally someplace else, not where our body is now: instead of paying full attention to our present activity, we're probably thinking about the meeting we've just left, the conversation we had last night, or the phone call we have to make in an hour. Or we're wondering what the kids are doing or what we should do about a friend's problem or whether the car will last another winter.

This is not to say that we shouldn't spend some productive time planning or analyzing things. But most of us spend hardly any time at all really being fully here in the present, where our body is. Even when we plan or analyze, our effectiveness is diminished because our attention and awareness are scattered then, too. Developing your inner willpower means pulling awareness and attention together in one place at one time. And that place is where your body is now.

The following experience break will allow you to let go of some of the mental distractions of the past or the future, and improve and expand your awareness of the present moment.

Inner Willpower Experience No. 2: The Path and the Present

Let's get a long view of the path ahead. Breathe easy and let your mind play. Just follow along; this is play, not an exam.

* * *

Begin by allowing yourself to enter the present moment. Look around: sense the stillness and peace of the place where you are sitting.

Allow yourself to become aware of your breathing. Just follow your breath gently: in, and out. Take your time.

Let go of the tensions and issues of the day. Feel them flowing away from you with your outward breath. Be here.

Close your eyes for a few moments if you prefer, and continue to focus on your breathing.

When you are ready, imagine for a moment that your life is a long country road. The road begins when you are born, and will end when you depart. It winds solidly away behind as you stand in its center, over territory you've passed through.

A somewhat mistier and floating path stretches out ahead of you into the future, over some scenic hills and valleys and out of sight into the distance. The future path becomes solid only as you step forward onto it. When you move to the left or the right, the newly created path moves with you.

Now imagine that you're in a magical hot-air balloon, or have the wings of a bird, or that you can simply float upward. Begin to drift up, up, and away, higher and higher in perfect safety, until the whole vast landscape and road is spread out below.

In your mind's eye, see the green hills and valleys, the empty desert, the mountains, and the rolling rivers that carried you along. See both the swampy places that bogged you down and tripped you up, and the firm, lush, comfortable ones that eased your way.

* * *

Look where your road winds through the past. That's a lot of territory you've covered, isn't it? See where your road was once only a dirt path? Remember those spots where it vanished entirely into the night? And you didn't know where to go next? From up here, it all seems so simple and obvious, doesn't it? It wasn't at the time, that's for sure.

From here, you can see that all those earlier goals and destinations—childhood dreams, making the team, first real job, first date, maybe first mortgage—weren't destinations at all, but merely signposts along the way. To where? The road continued; you moved on toward other goals. And what of them, now?

Look ahead, where the path is mistier and paler: The road doesn't end in the future either, does it? It is waiting to be created ahead of you, with each of your decisions, each of your steps. The road of your life is a process, you are always traveling further on, sometimes without being sure whether you're on any road at all.

Depending on your philosophical preference, you might even see that the road doesn't really end with this lifetime, but goes on in an unbroken line for many, many more lifetimes, always moving forward, always passing new signposts. If you feel, as Voltaire did, that it is no more remarkable that a man can be born many times than that he can be born once, this longer perspective may be somehow comforting, or perhaps more daunting. But even if your belief is confined to the journey of this present lifetime, it makes no difference from here: the need to continue onward remains the same. You can see that there is never any real arriving, only the continuous journey. Making this journey is what willpower is all about.

Drifting back here onto the ground into your comfortable chair, have another look around you and return to this present moment. Where are you now? This isn't a trick question: simply look around this familiar, comfortable room, and begin to appreciate that, after all those travels, and all those ups and downs along the way, the journey has brought you here, to this present moment. Right here. To this place at this time.

As you sit here in this present moment, you can understand that the past you saw in your imagination has dissolved. It vanished into the mists when you looked around the present room. The past is truly gone. Done. None of it exists except in your memory. Even this morning has dissolved, even ten minutes ago is no more. It's a wonderfully liberating thought, isn't it? You're free right now. You're sitting here in this room. Go ahead: grin and enjoy it.

And what about the future? It hasn't been created yet. Nothing has been determined. To be sure, some of the terrain has been mapped out since the creation of the universe, and that's what we call destiny. But the route you'll choose to take through it and the destinations (funny word, isn't it?) you'll pick are up to you. Whether you'll opt for a speedy race across the scorching, ascetic desert, tackle a mountain, or choose the more circuitous route through the scenic hills, that's your choice. Or, if you're feeling philosophical, that's your free will.

Each route will have its own advantages and disadvantages. Each will have to be dealt with on its own terms if you are to continue moving forward. But it's your choice.

What about all those wonderful hopes and plans and ideas you have for your future: those destinations and signposts you've chosen for your journey—how can you influence their realization? How can you create your future? How can you create that journey? Can you do it "in the future"? Can you really live one single second ahead of the present moment? No.

* * *

You can have hopes and dreams for the future, but all that you *really* have, and all that continuously travels with you, is this present moment. Right here. Now. In this room. The present moment is not simply holding a place between yesterday and tomorrow. It's all that there really is. This evolving moment is the sum total of reality and existence. It's absurdly simple, isn't it?

4
Everything You Need Is Here

When you bring yourself together in this present moment, you will find many things that you may not have noticed before, but foremost among them are the skills of your inner willpower: greater awareness, self-acceptance, the power to act, and the creative energy of affirmation.

Actually, you'll find that everything you need right now is here right now. Everything. You might be thinking that you really need a few thousand dollars right now, or at least a cigarette, and that everything is not here the way you'd like it to be, but take a closer look at this statement:

> Everything that you need right now is here right now.

The key words are "right now," in this present moment. Everything in your life—the sum total of your earlier life and all the seeds of your future life to be—is uniquely contained right here, hidden right in this moment. You might say that this moment, right now, is the outcome of everything that has gone before. And all of your future will evolve from this moment, right here.

It may seem odd, perhaps, that all those ups and downs along the way have added up to this time and place right here, but that's it. That's what it has all "meant": this. This room. This situation.

All of the tools—the means to create your solutions, and your future—are hidden here as well. You may at times feel that these tools are very well hidden indeed. But just as the answer is always contained in the question, the beginnings of your solution are present right here, wrapped in your situation.

Awareness Reveals Your Path

There is one simple skill that will allow you to see that everything you need for this present moment—including your inner willpower—is here now.

Awareness: the enhanced perception that comes with being fully here. Awareness enables you to understand your present situation more clearly. It allows you to make faster and easier progress toward your goal because it enables you to see what you are really dealing with. You need to know where you are before you can move forward productively.

For example, suppose you were going to visit a friend in an unfamiliar part of town. You have his address, but you get lost. Spotting a phone booth, you call him for directions. What's the first thing your friend will ask you? Of course: "Where are you now?"

Even when you know your destination and have all the help in the world, you can't get there from here until you know where "here" is. Then you can begin to make real progress. You'll know what you have to do next from where you are. Awareness is what tells you where you are. Otherwise, you'll keep trying to get to New York from Chicago, when you're actually in Miami. No wonder you can't seem to make any progress.

Awareness Focuses Your Energies

Everything you need for your inner willpower is here now because, by becoming aware, you've brought all your energies into one place at one time. Once you begin to focus those energies on what you need to do, that energy is sufficient for whatever action is called for at the moment. As we talk about the rest of the inner willpower skills, you'll discover how to strengthen the energy that you've brought into focus with awareness.

All that you ever really have to deal with or do is whatever is required right here in front of you, right now in any given moment.

Because this present moment moves and evolves and travels continuously with you, any given "right now" makes relatively small demands on you in terms of what is required within that moment to reach your goals, or to "do the right thing," or to use your inner willpower.

To use your inner willpower most effectively, you need only concern yourself with acting in the present, not in the past or in the future. Acting in the present is the only real way you can respond to the past that has brought you here, or to create the circumstances of your future.

"The longest journey begins with a single step," Lao Tzu said. This wise man understood that it does not matter how ambitious or modest your goal, or how near or far you may be from your destination. Each journey is accomplished in exactly the same way: by putting one foot in front of the other, by repeating a series of small steps again and again.

Each step, no matter how insignificant it may seem on its own, is actually the crucial step in moving you forward. Nothing can replace it. No amount of thinking or wishing or planning can replace action in the present for actually moving you forward. No matter how much you may yearn for your goal, or how earnestly you may gaze at it in the distance or in your dreams, the only thing that will actually get you there is contained in that humble little step waiting beneath your feet right now. Each step, no matter how small, is meaningful progress. Taking it is the only way you will ever get there from here.

Focus on the Path, Not the Goal

It's vital to have wonderful goals and priorities, but if you continually focus only on the end result and on the whole enormous journey ahead of you, you can quickly become overwhelmed and demoralized, even if you only want to get to the gym on Thursdays. The distance between where you are now and where you want to be can seem like the distance from here to the moon, and just as impossible to reach on foot. And, if you continue to look at the journey as though it were one enormous leap, it *is* impossible.

If you're going to learn the skills of inner willpower, you must learn the skills of action in the present moment. That means shifting the focus of your awareness into this present moment, away from your destination and toward the process of traveling itself.

It is the process of traveling, and not the destination itself that actually accomplishes meaningful change in your life. It is the process of traveling that is the true skill of inner willpower. Your destination is only a direction. Your success in attaining that destination lies in your continued progress along the way, one step at a time.

Using Everyday Awareness

You can begin to make use of your inner willpower by using your awareness to enhance your understanding of your present habits. It's important to begin to see yourself and your actions clearly, without making judgments or assessments. To see without responding to those feelings of fear, excitement, frustration, self-loathing, or nagging guilt that distort and prematurely close off your view of yourself and your world.

Even if you think that you already know far too much about your present condition and what you want to change, if you'll slow down long enough to use some applied awareness during your day, you can very quickly and painlessly gain a much firmer footing both within yourself and in your external situation. You'll begin to discover the inner strength and confidence that come with greater clarity.

To begin applying your awareness, experiment with this experience for ten minutes a day for the next few days.

Inner Willpower Experience No. 3: The Ten-Minute Blitz

Choose any behavior or habit that you'd like to change, whether it's related to your diet, health, personal relationships, organizational skills, or whatever aspect of your life you'd like to improve.

As you begin to do the familiar actions of this behavior, simply relax, enter the present moment, and become aware. Use the Present Moment Exercise, or any of those in the Appendix that you prefer.

Don't change anything. Just act as you usually do, but act with awareness.

Become aware of your body and your breathing. Notice exactly what your actions are, and how you feel as you do them. Be fully present; act with totality and commitment.

Become aware of any satisfaction or frustration that the activity holds for you. How much of this activity is actually pleasurable for you right now? How much of the pleasure was really in your anticipation or imagination or memory of some past encounter with this activity?

What is your awareness showing you?

At first, it may seem that the only thing your awareness is showing you is: there I go again. But if you persist with this little experiment, you may begin to notice other things about your behavior, like how much less "automatic" the habit becomes when you begin to perform it consciously. Or how far along into your habitual action you actually get without becoming aware. You might become aware of external cues or circumstances that initiate these automatic actions. You may realize that there are points in your behavior where you have greater control. Or that the activity no longer has any particular meaning for you.

Whatever you discover, continued awareness will begin to break up the monolithic, automatic nature of the behavior or habit, making it seem less onerous and unyielding.

Awareness Frees You

You may initially respond with disappointment to the apparent dominance of the habit in your life. This doesn't mean that increased awareness is about to plunge you into a horror show called Facing Reality: a world of dire ugliness, inadequacy, and disgusting personal habits. You aren't as awful as all that. And chances are, you've already got a pretty good idea of what the most unappetizing aspects of your behavior really are anyway.

But even if it hurts to see something, it helps free you. Seeing something as it is can release you from fear and pain. Have you ever had friends or colleagues who were going through a period of great uncertainty in their life? Perhaps their job was iffy, or their marriage was rocky, or someone's health was in question. And then, finally, the thing is settled: the job's gone, or the marriage is over. The news is bad, but done is done. What happens to your friends' energy? They seem suddenly liberated from a tremendous psychic burden, don't they? Some great emotional weight seems to lift from them, even though their external situation may have become much more difficult.

What has helped your friends? Knowing the outcome; knowing where they are. Knowing what you have to deal with means you're no longer frittering away energy on worry and fear, fighting an imaginary situation in your mind. It's been said that 90 percent of finding the solution lies in defining the problem. When the situation becomes more defined, you know what needs to be done. Being able to see something as it is can be a tremendous relief.

Awareness doesn't only work in negative life situations. Awareness also enhances your pleasure, sensuality, and aesthetic appreciation. The crunch of a salad or the softness of a chair are waiting to entertain you, if you're aware of them. Simply walking in the sunshine, enjoying the colors of a passing shop window, or listening to the distant laughter of children can add unexpected benefits to your day.

Most people, for instance, eat simply because it's mealtime or because there's food available, and end up having far too much of something they didn't really want or actually need. Awareness can help you gain control of your meals very quickly, and it can make your daily fare much more enjoyable as well as healthful.

Here's how to apply awareness to your everyday meals:

* * *

Inner Willpower Experience No. 4: The Premeal Body Checkout

Several minutes or a half hour before eating your next meal, and before there is any food in sight, begin to increase your awareness of the present moment by focusing your attention on your breathing.

Use your favorite Present Moment Exercise to bring yourself more fully into the here and now.

Become aware of your body as you sit or stand. How does it feel right now? How are you breathing? Simply notice, without changing anything. What's your energy level like right now? What's happening inside of you? How do you feel? Become aware.

Now become aware of your midsection and your appetite, your feelings of hunger or fullness. How hungry is your body—really—right now? Is it still mostly satisfied from your previous meal? Or are you eager to devour anything that's not nailed down? What does your body say?

Are you about to eat just because it's mealtime and you expect to eat, or do you want to eat because you're hungry? Are you eating now because you're afraid of being hungry a few hours from now? What's really going on with your appetite right here and now?

What, if anything, would your body like to eat? What would feel right? What kind of foods? Something solid and hearty? Something light and fresh? Hot? Cold? Sweet? Salty? Creamy? Fruity? Are you more thirsty than hungry? Are you truly undecided—or simply uninterested in food right now? Listen to your body.

* * *

If you're hungry and could choose anything in the world right now, what appeals to you the most? Let the answer come from your body's awareness, not your imagination or the menu or the contents of your refrigerator. Feel what your body is really telling you to eat before you begin choosing your food.

Act accordingly.

Notice how awareness begins to modify your choices, or the amount that you may choose to eat. The amount of food you consume may temporarily increase when you begin using this experience, but continued awareness will eventually bring your diet into a normal, healthful range that's appropriate for your body and your lifestyle.

INCREASING YOUR DIET POWER

You can use awareness to enhance the effectiveness of your nutritional program or diet. My friend Margaret, for instance, was facing a drastic change in her diet and lifestyle. Her most recent medical checkup had brought a disturbing warning from her doctor: her cholesterol scores and blood pressure were dangerously high. It was time to change her eating habits or face the consequences.

She smiled wanly as I sat down to join her for lunch. "How am I going to change my whole life and stay on this diet forever? I don't have that much willpower!"

I told her: Let's not worry about your whole life yet; you're only here to have lunch. All you have to do right now is put together and enjoy a healthful and satisfying meal. The rest of your life will come later.

I suggested that she might want to put aside her preconceived ideas about what to order and use the Premeal Body Checkout instead.

"Well, now that I pay attention," Margaret said, "I guess I'm not really famished right now. But I'd like something hot and tasty. Hmmm . . ." She scoured the menu. "Hearty vegetable minestrone soup. That would hit the spot. And some freshly baked bread and a salad." By becoming aware of what her body wanted, Margaret was able to select something satisfying as well as healthy.

The next awareness technique can help you *while* you are eating. Here's how you do it:

Inner Willpower Experience No. 5: Eating with Awareness

Before starting your meal, bring yourself into the present moment: become aware of the place where you are seated to eat. Look around; notice the space that you are in. See the colors, the shapes, and the textures. Notice the qualities of the light, and of the air. Listen to the sounds. Relax and enjoy being seated where you are.

Become aware of your body. Feel how you are seated on your chair; feel the surface of the chair as it supports your body.

Become aware of the foods on your plate. Enjoy the arrangement of colors and shapes on the plate, the aromas and textures. Appreciate for a moment how much loving energy went into preparing this meal for you. Feel your body's anticipation of a pleasant meal.

If you are practicing a special diet or wish to improve your nutrition, look at each of the foods on your plate and appreciate their special health-giving and nutritional qualities. Use your knowledge of good nutrition—whatever it may be—to become more aware of the vitamins, minerals, enzymes, fiber, and other beneficial elements your body is about to enjoy. Think about how this meal will contribute to your health, energy, and well-being.

Also become aware of those elements on your plate that do not promote your body's well-being. Simply become aware of them; note what those ingredients are, how much is on your plate, and where they are.

Take up a spoonful or forkful and taste the food. Become aware of the first sensations of flavor, aroma, and texture as you bite into the food. Notice the way it feels in your mouth, how the flavor spreads throughout your palate as you chew the first mouthful. Remain in the present moment, savoring this first taste as long as you can. Really taste it. Take your time.

Now continue enjoying each mouthful with the same awareness.

After you have eaten a bit, notice how your sensations of taste and texture have changed from your first mouthful. Does the food still taste as good, or are you eating mechanically to clean the plate? Notice how your body's response to the food is beginning to change.

After you've eaten half or three-quarters of what's on your plate, check in with your body again: How hungry are you now? What is your body telling you? Become aware of the changes since you began your meal.

Finish your meal in accordance with your awareness: eat while you are hungry; stop when you are full.

When you've finished your meal, take a moment to appreciate how diligently your body's digestive system will work for the next few hours to turn your food into life-giving energy and health.

❖

"Mmmm," Margaret sighed as we finished our main course, "if this is awareness, it certainly helps me enjoy my meal more. I didn't realize that inner willpower had so much to do with the senses."

"But I can see your point," she continued. "Becoming more involved with where I am makes it harder to get distracted by where I'm not. That makes things easier, doesn't it? Except . . ." Her face fell suddenly. "I just remembered their famous Italian ice cream. They make a decadent nougat here."

She looked at me intently. "What am I going to do? I can't face life without ever having the rich foods I love. But they're like poison for me now. . . ."

I asked her whether her doctor had told her she could never have any. "Not exactly. But he said I've got to really cut back. It feels like the same awful thing."

"Sounds like you need to choose an inner willpower project to get you started," I replied. She raised an inquiring eyebrow, then began to smile.

"Tell me about it while I have some of the ice cream."

An inner willpower project, I explained, was a simple way to begin to integrate the Inner Willpower Experiences into your daily life.

"Oh brother," she moaned. "I've got a zillion projects I could be doing if only I had the willpower. . . ."

This is how you'll get the willpower, I replied. An inner willpower project is specially selected for the precise purpose of enhancing your willpower skills. It's the next step in the process of inner willpower.

5
Beginning Your Own Inner Willpower Program

Your inner willpower project is a tool for learning. It is a modest undertaking that can provide you with fifteen to thirty minutes per day of willpower learning time. It's a testing field or playground for trying out the inner willpower skills you'll be learning in this book as you go, and acts as an important complement to the text.

Your project will act as a mirror for you, giving you instant feedback on your progress. With it, you'll be able to apply the techniques presented here in a practical fashion, follow along throughout the book with your own solid experience, and gain valuable insights into the ways that inner willpower works for you. You'll be able to learn as you go, applying the skills from this book to your project as you learn them.

Because willpower is an experience, your project will give you plenty of opportunity to gain high-potency experience in its easiest and most accessible form. You'll be able to shape your inner willpower to meet your own needs by developing it on a project of your own choosing.

Willpower is a set of skills. Your project will help you learn how to use them and to become comfortable with them in a manageable, no-lose setting where you can experiment and use trial-and-error learning, the same way you'd go about learning any other valuable skills.

When you learned to walk, you started by learning to crawl and to stand upright. When you fell over, you probably laughed, and got right back up and tried again. You didn't care about "failure," so it couldn't stop you.

But when we set out to do something that we think "takes willpower"—like exercising regularly, improving nutrition, or cutting back on or getting started on or finishing something—we somehow expect ourselves to be able to do it perfectly, without ever missing a day, right from the start. Even worse, if we can't do it perfectly, we often won't do it at all.

If you stop to think about any of your favorite skills, whether it's whipping up a gourmet meal or running a computer or even a corporate department, you'll remember that there was a time when you were just beginning. And if you'd been asked to do back then what you can do so confidently today, you might have felt inept, terrified, and totally frustrated. You might even have given up and walked away from it entirely back then, and never accomplished anything, because the task would have seemed so overwhelming and incomprehensible.

But you were willing to learn. You gradually got better at it.

The peaks and valleys of your accomplishment don't matter as much after a while as the level of your overall consistency: How good are you at doing whatever it is, most of the time, on any average day? How much skill do you have that you can count on, no matter what you're feeling like or what's going on around you? That's what matters when it comes to inner willpower, too.

Improving that level of willpower consistency is what your inner willpower project is for. Gradually getting better and better at doing what you want to do until you can do it no matter how you are feeling, or whatever else is going on around you, is what mastering your inner willpower is all about.

Choosing a Good Project

The best inner willpower project is one that:

- *You have an opportunity to do every day,* like walking the last five blocks to work, or having a serving of vegetables—any kind—with your dinner, or doing ten minutes of stretching before settling down to watch television. A daily opportunity will allow you to learn inner willpower skills much faster than something you do only once or twice a week.
- *Is simple and feasible:* something you can reasonably fit into your present schedule and lifestyle. A small project, like a twenty-minute walk, is just as valuable for learning as a two-hour workout.
- *Requires a physical action,* like eating something healthy, walking, cycling, stretching, phoning, writing, or cleaning. A physical activity completes the inner willpower learning process, gives you rapid and clear feedback on your learning, and holds the inherent satisfaction of accomplishment. Physical activity will forge a tangible link for you between your intentions and your actions, the link that is so often missing when we think we "need willpower."

The need for a positive physical action makes denial projects impractical as learning tools. This means—for right now—no projects that involve giving something up, swearing off anything, forgoing, skipping, or anything that includes the words "never," "I won't," or "I quit." At this stage, focus on saying "I will." Later on, when we talk about the inner willpower skill of conscious action, you'll learn how to use positive activity to cut back or drop unwanted habits: you'll learn the secret of "won't power." For right now, let's focus on the basics.

Some possible projects might be:

- If you're thinking about improving your fitness level, how about a half-hour walk around the block before or after dinner? Or fifteen minutes of gentle stretching before bedtime?
- If you already belong to a fitness club, how about simply showing up, and spending twenty minutes on your choice of equipment, or just taking a sauna. The important thing here is just to show up—not how much you do when you get there.
- If you feel messy and disorganized, how about fifteen minutes of picking up any kind of loose debris in your home or office in the morning or evening? You'll notice I said fifteen minutes, not a whole hour's blitz.
- If you'd like to return phone calls or answer letters more quickly, how about setting aside a half hour when you come into your office or before lunch for returning as many calls as you can make in that half hour—no more than that? Or pick up just one letter and scribble a reply. Stop when the half hour is up.
- If improving your nutrition is your goal, think about *adding* something nutritious to your daily menu, like whole grains or a piece of fresh fruit (any kind), or a salad, or some fish. Do not—repeat, do not—consider eliminating anything just yet. Keep your usual diet, ice cream and all. Eat as much as you usually eat. You're going to focus on making just one of those things an item from your chosen category, that's all.
- Be creative. Your choice is entirely personal.

* * *

What You'll Learn

When you get this first project under control—which may take several weeks or even months—you'll have learned a great deal about the basic skills of inner willpower: awareness, self-acceptance, conscious action, and creative affirmation. And you'll have learned how to apply them in a practical way. You'll find that expanding your project, or taking the next step toward your goal, is infinitely easier once you have some real inner willpower skills to call on.

The daily nature of your project will help you to build toward a degree of consistency in your actions. That means that you aren't going to try to be perfect all at once. Instead you'll gradually improve your average until you can actually do what you choose to do most of the time, at least as pertains to your daily project.

If, for instance, you'd like to stop procrastinating about returning phone calls or letters, you might choose a project that consists of spending twenty minutes each day before lunch returning however many calls you can return in that time. No more, no less. Any that don't get completed can wait until the next day before lunch. Any days that you don't return any, don't count.

You may find that you'll start out actually making these calls only about 10 or 20 percent of the time, maybe not much better than you're doing now. Maybe even worse. No matter. You'll use this as a chance to experiment with your inner willpower skills, and as you learn, your average will gradually improve.

Pretty soon you'll be returning your calls maybe 60 or 70 percent of the time, and feeling much more self-confident about your ability to determine your behavior, and to act according to your choices. Eventually you may be able to say that you return 80 or 90 percent of your calls within twenty-four hours.

At that point, whether or not you'll care about being "perfect," and never, ever delaying or dropping a call, will become an academic rather than a practical issue. Instead, you'll probably be applying your new inner willpower skills to something else that you want to do, like updating the sales reports more promptly, or starting your vacation planning earlier, or just doing the dishes or laundry on most days. You'll be focused on getting better, not on being "perfect."

Avoiding the Perfect Trap

Expecting to be perfect is one of the sneakiest traps there is. It can very often stop you cold before you've even begun.

Take Fred, for instance. He'd begun working out at his health club, signing up for everything, and planning to spend two hours every evening exercising. He quit after two months, and now sat patting his belt buckle ruefully.

"I know I've got to get back to it, but it's such a big commitment. Besides, it's too late for me; I haven't gone back in months!"

Fred imagined that he had to work out for two hours every night—or not at all. When he couldn't live up to his unrealistic expectations for himself, he let himself off the hook by doing nothing.

I suggested to him that it had taken him maybe fifteen years to get *out* of shape. He couldn't expect to get back together overnight, and he should give himself time to grow back into it. Otherwise, he'd only get discouraged.

"Yeah," he nodded. "I guess that's what happened. I tried to do too much. Funny, you know: I'm always telling the people in my department to be realistic with their estimates. I guess I should apply that to myself."

Fred had fallen into the trap. Instead of seeing regular workouts as a goal that he could work toward, he saw them as an all-or-nothing deal. And he settled for nothing instead of meaningful progress toward something. Without realizing it, he had set himself up for defeat.

MAKING YOURSELF A GOOD DEAL

In choosing how you will begin to work on anything that you think "requires willpower," it's important to choose something that is actually possible for you to do under your present circumstances, assuming that you want to do it. Use practicality—Can I actually live with this on a long-term basis?—as a criterion for choosing your inner willpower project. You might not, realistically, be able to visit your health club every night after work, but maybe you could set Tuesday evenings aside for some "club time." At some point in the future, you might be able to add Thursdays or Saturdays, but for right now, focus on getting to your health club on most Tuesdays.

Or you might decide to take a stroll each evening after dinner, and work on that, instead of telling yourself you're going to jog vigorously every morning before breakfast.

Look for a project that you'll enjoy and get some inherent satisfaction out of doing. Work from love, not fear. Learning inner willpower is not a question of pain, or testing yourself against some unrealistic standard. It's a matter of learning how to expand your "comfort zone"—that range of activities that feels comfortable and natural—and how to do those things that you really want to do. Later on, you'll be able to apply your increased inner willpower skills to more demanding circumstances and creative challenges, with love and a sense of natural balance.

A good project may seem almost too easy. Perhaps you'd like to really get your teeth into something. Believe me, a simple project can prove to be plenty challenging when you begin to put it into practice on a daily basis. Remember, it's daily consistency that you're shooting for, not occasional heroism. You can always expand your project as you go.

There's Always Something

It's important, at the same time, not to talk yourself into believing that, under your unique circumstances—say, work pressures, your family situation, a client's needs, a bad back, or tight finances—you cannot do anything at all right now. The simple truth is that no matter what you are thinking of doing, if you look for the restrictions and the reasons why not, you can always find good ones. And the more you look, the more you can find. There's never going to be a time when absolutely everything is 100 percent in your favor. Restrictions are a fact of life.

But if you think about it, you'll notice that whenever you are able to do what you want to do, whether it's simply going shopping instead of working around the house, or something major, like changing jobs or residences, there are usually reasons why you still "can't." But the difference is that you've decided you want to do it anyway. So you do it. We'll talk more about motivation and priorities, but for right now it's enough to understand that external restrictions or circumstances are not always what they seem. And that even the most "difficult" limitations will eventually yield to slow, gradual change on your part.

Don't allow yourself to be fooled into "I can't, because . . ." Just do what you can. There is always *something* that is possible under your present circumstances. Change doesn't always happen in the way that you think it will. The route to your destination may bend one way or another to avoid an obstacle or follow a path of least resistance. But it will take you where you want to go if you are willing to keep at it.

Fred, when I caught up with him a few weeks later, was in an upbeat mood.

"I've thought about my workouts," he said, "and decided that I really enjoy swimming, not lifting weights. So I've started visiting the pool before I go home, just to do a few laps. I've only got about enough energy for five laps, but it sure feels good.

"But you know what? Instead of telling myself how much I'll swim," he added, "I'm focusing on just getting myself to the locker room and into my trunks. That's enough of a project right now."

I agreed. As that eminent contemporary philosopher Woody Allen once observed, 90 percent of the secret of life lies in just showing up.

DEVELOPING YOUR INNER TALENT

But Fred had another question: "Isn't willpower just something other people are born with? It's a talent: you either have it or you don't, right?"

Not exactly, I replied. Even the greatest natural talent will never amount to anything unless it's developed with plenty of practice. Mozart, I pointed out, may have composed his first symphony when he was eight years old, but by that age he'd already written dozens of lesser pieces and spent thousands of hours at the keyboard. He had talent, but talent alone didn't make him great.

We've all seen the flip side of talent as well: the brilliant person who never applied himself—and who never went anywhere. Talent alone cannot predict the outcome, but practice and dedication can. If two people have the same goal, and person A has lots of talent and little willingness to work, and person B has less talent but will work like crazy at it—which one do you think will go further?

You could have lots of dormant willpower talent. But you'll never know if you don't give it a chance to develop. The secret to any skill—even willpower—is found in its doing. And that's what your project is all about.

6
Living with Your Project—and Yourself

By now you've chosen a few minutes during your ordinary day that you can use to practice your inner willpower skills. You're ready to begin making real progress.

So far, you've experienced the ability to enter more fully into the present moment, which is the key to all four inner willpower skills, and the first skill, awareness.

For right now, use your daily project time to focus on becoming better at entering the present moment easily and naturally. When the time of day comes to begin your inner willpower project, take as much time as you need to make the essential connection with your inner core of centeredness and balance. Don't hesitate to refer back to Chapter 2 as frequently as you want to. In the weeks ahead you'll probably find that you can slip into the present moment with increasing ease and subtlety, in the space of only a few relaxed breaths.

An Unexpected Benefit: Meditation

At the same time, perhaps you'll find that learning to enter the present moment leads quite naturally to a state of meditation, an inner experience of stillness and harmony that is profoundly rewarding in its own right. You may very well discover that this magnificent skill is emerging via the Present Moment Exercise, and that on those days when you reach a meditative state you prefer to prolong the time you spend simply sitting in a state of inner stillness.

If the pleasures of meditation appeal to you on these occasions, you will discover that you can quite easily deepen and enhance this experience by simply closing your eyes and continuing to focus on your breath as it enters and leaves your nostrils. Allow yourself to respond naturally, and without forcing, to any subtle changes in your breathing or posture that meditation brings. This is Mother Nature's way of recharging your batteries and allowing your body's flow of energy to realign itself.

When you are ready to continue with your day, simply become aware again of your body and your breathing. Take a deep breath, allow your eyes to open, stretch a little if you'd like. Flow naturally toward the next thing you need to do in your inner willpower program.

You will find that your awareness, clarity, and energy level dramatically increase on these occasions, and that any work you do on your inner willpower skills, after you've completed a few minutes of meditation, becomes powerfully enhanced and meaningful. You'll make rapid progress if you take the time to enter the present moment as fully as you can.

Many people find the skill of meditation so helpful to other areas of their life that they enjoy setting aside a few minutes in the early morning or before bed for the pleasures of meditation alone. If you enjoy meditation, congratulations and best wishes. You've gained a priceless inner treasure that will serve you well in the years to come.

The benefits of being in the present moment may begin to emerge in many seemingly unrelated areas of your life, and you may find that working on your inner willpower skills is bringing you unanticipated bonuses in the form of fresh solutions and insights into other situations, improved personal energy, inner confidence, and satisfaction.

When the Moment Falls Flat

There will be days when, in spite of your best efforts, entering the present moment may seem elusive. In contrast to the joyous stillness you may previously have experienced, the sense of the present may seem ordinary or flat. This is natural, and absolutely nothing to be concerned about.

If you have gone through the steps to entering the present moment, you are in the best possible state, regardless of how you may subjectively feel about it. Your experience will vary from day to day, because you yourself are different from moment to moment. Do not expect today's experience to repeat yesterday's. Just remain aware, carry on, and flow along with the experience. You are exactly where you are supposed to be.

Entering the present moment may also become less dramatic because, as you continue to become more acquainted with the present, you'll naturally begin to spend more time fully here in the moment as you go through your day, whether or not you are actively aware of it. Using the Present Moment Exercise has a cumulative benefit that helps your energies to become more focused throughout the day. It does not end when you finish the exercise.

Understanding Your Own Obstacles

You'll probably also find that one of the first things your awareness will begin showing you as you approach the time for your inner willpower project is a million reasons why you "can't" do it today. Obstacles of all kinds, large and small, will begin emerging.

Using awareness, you can begin to actually see and experience these obstacles for what they are: obstructions that you place in your own path. These can appear in the form of excuses and fears, aches, pains, sudden fatigue, other appointments, or a need for an urgent trip to the refrigerator or supermarket when the time for your inner willpower project arrives.

Samantha, for instance, is a would-be screenwriter. Her first script, though, has yet to be committed to paper. Using awareness, she began to find that when the time came for her to sit down at her word processor, she'd develop a fervent interest in doing the laundry or phoning a friend "first." Or she'd sit down and immediately spring up to make a cup of coffee or adjust the cushions "just to get comfortable."

"At first I thought it was no wonder that I could never get my writing done when there were so many other things I needed to do," she said. "And then I began to get annoyed that such trivial things kept coming up.

"But I just remained aware, and watched myself moving from evasion to evasion. I just kept doing each one with awareness, even if they used up my entire inner willpower time for the day.

"I began to see that, each time, I was really making a choice about my actions, and part of me welcomed the intrusions because they'd let me off the hook for a few minutes.

"Excuses keep arising as long as I keep focusing on them. I've really begun to see what I'm doing to myself," Samantha concluded.

Inner and Outer Obstacles

There are two kinds of obstacles: internal and external. Internal obstacles have something to do with your physical or emotional state, such as feeling a cold coming on, a headache, or a sense of boredom, frustration, lingering anger, or annoyance directed at someone else. It may be a fear of running out of time to "do it properly" or "not feeling up to it today," or of neglecting some other task or appointment.

An excuse can take a very external form. That is, it frequently appears to result from some external circumstance or the needs of someone else, such as the need to return a phone call, or to be somewhere else, or the fear that one's spouse or partner will be annoyed.

Many married couples find spouses are an invariably convenient way to turn a so-so internal excuse into a more plausible external one: "I'd love to, but *he'd* be angry" or "but *she* won't let me." That may be, but in many cases you'll find that saying so also conveniently lets you off the hook. If you feel secretly relieved or happy that your spouse or partner or another person is an obstacle and that you are now "unfortunately" free to continue some self-destructive behavior, that's a pretty good sign that you've taken an internal excuse and externalized it. In other words, you've placed an obstacle for yourself right where you want it.

CUTTING OBSTACLES DOWN TO SIZE

Does this mean that these excuses or obstacles aren't "real" and that they can be quietly ignored? It depends. They're as real as anything else on the physical or emotional level. And they need to be dealt with in the same practical way.

Right now, it isn't necessary for you to understand or even believe your own role in creating these obstacles. Simply allow yourself to keep an open mind about how much influence you may actually have over your own life and your own experiences.

From the perspective of your enhanced awareness and ability to live in the present moment, though, begin to respond to each obstacle as a choice, and act freely right here in the present moment. Begin to do whatever is necessary to deal with each obstacle just as it is, no more, no less.

You may choose to stop and take care of the obstacle. Or you might simply ignore it. The only rule is that you use your best judgment under the circumstances, remaining aware of what the obstacle is, and aware of how you are responding to it.

Even if you believe you have absolutely nothing to do with what comes to you, you always—always—have the choice about how you will respond. The elusive "free will" of philosophers is simply your ability to choose, your ability to use your judgment, your ability to respond according to your personal priorities and values.

No matter how "driven" you may feel by your emotions, fears, hopes, or physical needs, you can still make choices about how you will respond to both your inner and outer circumstances. Continued awareness will allow you to remain comfortably at the center of your inner self, able to draw on your energies as you need them.

Fred Steers His Own Course

Fred found that his decision to get to the swimming pool after work began to bring up a number of external obstacles that seemed ideally crafted to play on his personal fears of career success.

"At the end of the day, there always seemed to be one more urgent thing that required my time. I'd normally leave about six-thirty, but I found that if I was going to the pool, something else always seemed to come up," Fred said.

How had he dealt with this?, I asked.

"I'm getting a little better about using the present moment—at least during my 'project' time—so I find that I feel more relaxed and don't get tossed off course as easily. I feel more comfortable about dealing with things on a case by case basis: Could it wait until morning? Could I take it home? Could I go to the pool later?

"I'm actually making it to the locker room two or three nights a week, though," he said proudly. "It feels good, too."

"Funny thing, though," he added. "As I began to feel more comfortable in my own mind with going to the pool, the disturbances seemed to fall away. I just began taking them in stride, and going swimming afterward anyway."

Fred had learned the very valuable skill of remaining "centered" in the present moment. Like a good sailor in command of his craft, he was able to adjust his sails according to the wind and the weather without changing his ideas about what course he wished to pursue.

Tailoring Your Project to Fit You

It is both necessary and wise to make adjustments to your project as needed, and as the demands of your day require. The important thing is to find a way to do *something* toward your project, and to reward yourself for any activity at all, even if you feel you are only going through the motions or not doing as much as you "should."

Doing something means:

- Take your walk before dinner instead of after if you find that it fits your schedule better. Don't feel tied to a time that isn't effective for you.
- Just stand up and do one stretch instead of fifteen minutes' worth. Begin to make the link to action in the present. You can always increase the amount later.
- Buy some oranges. Even if you don't eat one it still counts.
- Just go to the front door and take a few deep breaths, or wander down to the end of the driveway instead of taking your walk.
- Sort through your phone messages and pick the one that you would call if you were going to call anybody that day.

- Reduce your project to the absolute minimum activity required. Work on that.
- Find out what works for you. Be flexible, keep experimenting.

And on those days when nothing happens, nothing happens. At the end of your project time, just let it go and carry on with your day. Don't waste energy on guilt, worry, or recriminations. They can't help you. Remain aware. Focus on your progress. Tomorrow is a fresh opportunity. You're still learning.

7

Self-Acceptance: Working from Security, Not Fear

"I just keep procrastinating! And the more I put things off, the worse I feel. It doesn't seem to matter that I've become more aware of this: I still can't get any writing done. I feel like a worm."

Samantha, the screenwriter, was on the phone, in tears.

It was time, I suggested, for her to learn more about the second skill of inner willpower: self-acceptance.

Like many people, once Samantha had become aware of her behavior, she expected to leap right in and begin making changes. It's great to have so much enthusiasm for change, but there's actually a critical skill that comes after awareness, and before action.

That second willpower skill is self-acceptance: gaining inner strength by coming to terms with where you actually are, without squirming and struggling, without hating or rejecting yourself, without feeling guilty, worthless, or hopeless. Self-acceptance means loving yourself just for being you, lumps and all.

Self-Hatred Traps You

Self-acceptance is a tall order. It doesn't happen all at once. It's much easier just to hate yourself for leaving the laundry undone or the gym class unattended, or to mentally flog yourself for whatever you ate or drank or did last night.

Somehow, we keep thinking that if only we'd hate something enough—some aspect of ourselves, our appearance, or our behavior—it would give us the energy to propel us into changing. This is rarely the case.

Hatred and self-rejection may give you an initial jolt of energy, but once the first impact has worn off, it soon settles into a kind of frozen, immobile bitterness that requires a great deal of psychic and emotional energy to maintain. The energy we invest in self-hatred actually continues to freeze us, inhibits our actions, and restricts our ability to change into a better person.

It is one of Mother Nature's laws that concentrating on something gives it real psychic energy to interact with you, so guilt and self-rejection only succeed in giving energy to your weaknesses, fixing them even more strongly in your psyche. We may hope to gain energy from what we hate in order to move away from it, but actually we become trapped by hating something, since we must remain emotionally close to what we hate in order to continue getting the energy from that hatred. The more you hate yourself—for whatever reason—the more firmly you are tied to what you hate. And that's not a good way to move forward and make changes in your life.

Love Is Freeing

Love, on the other hand—including love of your own self as one of the natural creatures of this planet—is freeing. It is mobile, it is dynamic, it is laughter and dancing. It promotes healing and growth and life. It lives within you every minute, waiting to be tapped.

When you love yourself—in spite of certain traits you may want to change—just for being you, you give yourself a very solid emotional base to build on, a central core of unshakable strength, comfort, and security.

Loving yourself, and whatever you want to become, gives you energy that works like a magnet to draw you toward your goal. At first it may seem weaker than the jolt of self-hatred that comes when you are emotionally close to your weaknesses, but it is working from the opposite direction. As you begin to make progress and move closer to your goal and your inner strengths, the magnetic pull of whatever you love will become stronger, carrying you along over a far greater distance.

Self-acceptance is a vital inner willpower skill. It consolidates your energies in a positive fashion and frees you from unnecessary emotional burdens. When you're no longer fighting against yourself, you bring all your energies together. You become centered and focused, free to act with the awareness and insight that you've gained.

Masking the truth about your behavior forces you to spend energy to create and maintain a whole mental web of unintegrated information and pretext that is always in conflict with who you really are. With self-acceptance, you can bring much more power to your choices and actions.

The Experience of Self-Acceptance

This experience break will help you gain some practical experience in self-acceptance.

Inner Willpower Experience No. 6: The Inner Reconciliation

Retreat to your comfortable, private place where you can sit undisturbed for the next few minutes. As you read this, close your eyes whenever you need to in order to appreciate the experience. There is no need to rush.

Make yourself comfortable; sit quietly. Notice the silence that hangs pleasantly in the air around you, a soft protective zone between you and the outer world beyond. Glance slowly around the room; see how the silence flows easily over the surfaces of everything, spreading your secure, protected zone outward in all directions. Sit comfortably at its center.

Take that long, slow deep breath that your body needs. Breathe in the fresh, peaceful air, and let the tensions and stresses of the day flow outward and away, dissolving as they reach the floor. Continue breathing slowly and naturally, without forcing, allowing tiredness and staleness to flow out with each outward breath.

When you feel that your body has begun to relax, continue to free it by paying attention to each incoming breath. Feel the rejuvenating freshness of each breath; feel how it energizes each cell. Continue as long as you'd like. This is your personal time.

Now, in your imagination, allow yourself to be in a quiet place, under the shade of a large tree on a grassy hilltop in the country. It is a sunny summer afternoon; the air is mild and sweet. The grass underneath is soft and fragrant; the afternoon is calm and peaceful. Butterflies hover nearby. Take your time. Experience this place.

Lie down comfortably beneath the dappled shade of your tree. Allow yourself to feel the tender green grass as it envelops you, the warm earth as it cradles and supports you securely and gently.

* * *

Sink into the soft grass. Let go. Close your eyes and spend a few moments here. There's no place to go, nothing to do or be. Enjoy the timeless peace of a summer's afternoon.

As you lie quietly, gaze upward at the leafy, sunny branches overhead. Begin to drift upward, floating toward the branches, and through them, upward, until you are floating above the vast, green countryside, drifting higher and higher in perfect comfort.

Float upward until you are among the fluffy, peaceful clouds drifting serenely above the meadows. Settle in here, on your private cloud miles and miles above the distant, quiet countryside.

You may stay here as long as you like. Feel the inner peace and freedom that flows through your breathing now, the joy and harmony that arises naturally from the core of your being. Be at ease here.

There is someone, now, with whom your love energy flows naturally. In your mind's eye, see this person whom you truly love. Bring them here, before you, and welcome them. Experience the flow of love and peacefulness between you. Experience the joy of seeing your loved one again.

Feel the joy of this love flowing now throughout your body and around you. Feel how it delights you, warms you, cheers you, softens you. Feel how each cell of your body is smiling and bright with love's gentle glow.

Allow yourself to experience this light of love. Allow your light and love to flow to the other person. See this person surrounded by the gentle glow of your love. Take your time.

* * *

There are others whom you love. See each of them, now. Bring each of them here; bring them all here together. Extend the glow of your love to them. Feel how easily your love expands to include all of them. Feel how easily it can continue to expand, becoming deeper and more real.

Feel the strength and security of this love within you. Feel its comfort, its nourishment, its serenity. Feel how it belongs to you. Close your eyes and enjoy this experience.

There is someone else, now, with whom your love energy is blocked. Perhaps there has been a disagreement, a misunderstanding. Bring this person here in your mind's eye, too.

See this other person, now, from the light of your heart. See their pain, their confusion, their sincerity.

Let them be at peace now, let them understand. Allow the peace in your heart to extend as a soft glow to their heart. Take your time.

Say everything now that you have to say to them. Let the words flow from your heart, very quietly.

When you have finished, sit quietly and let them speak, too. Listen from the security of your inner core: what the other person has to say may surprise you. Close your eyes gently.

Allow yourself, from here, to forgive them. Forgive them and let them go, perhaps with an embrace, perhaps with a gift of light from your heart. Return to the security and serenity of your cloud. Be at peace.

Now, you have one more person to forgive: yourself. Yes, your own self. Allow your tenderness and compassion to flow here, too, to the one person who has suffered the most from your rejection.

Forgive yourself for all that has happened, for all that you've done, knowingly or unknowingly. Take your time. Be gentle with yourself.

Let the clear waters of mercy flow through you now, washing away all misunderstandings, all regrets. Let them go.

Be at peace. Experience this present moment as fully as you wish. Close your eyes.

When you're ready to return, gently begin breathing more deeply. Come back into your body, awaken and sit up slowly.

Look around the room where you've been sitting, reading this. How do you feel now? What's changed? What's new? Give yourself a hug.

Welcome Home

This is the experience of self-acceptance. This exercise made it a little easier, psychologically, by first enabling you to forgive and accept others and then to forgive yourself. Granted, what you have experienced here is probably more dramatic than you'll feel in day-to-day self-acceptance because of the large number of issues from the past you've quite possibly dealt with here. But now that they're gone, they're gone.

The underlying principle, that of extending love and forgiveness to yourself, is the core experience of self-acceptance. Isn't it remarkable how much hatred and rejection we can unknowingly inflict upon ourselves? Nobody outside of us does it to us—we do it to ourselves. Self-acceptance is a very powerful antidote.

What happens when you begin to love and accept yourself? It's quite astounding: lost, rejected parts of your inner self that have been crying somewhere out in the cosmos come home again, happy to be accepted back, ready to love you in return. It's an experience of being made whole, of integration and oneness with your true nature. Self-acceptance brings you back to you, the real person you've lost somewhere by unwittingly rejecting and hating parts of yourself.

THE EGO AND THE BUSINESS OF "LOVE"

Some people might say: "But love of yourself isn't *nice!* You're supposed to be thinking of others! You're being so egotistical, so self-centered, so narcissistic . . . !" This can arise from an honest misunderstanding about what kind of love we're talking about here.

Love in its lower, more primitive form comes from the ego, and is essentially possessive in nature. The ego—more or less—defines the boundaries of our individual personality, and the ego's "love" is devoted to enhancing itself. So the ego places conditions on what, and under what circumstances, it will "love" something or someone. It's the ego that says: "I love you because . . . , I would love you more if you . . . , After all I've done for you . . . !"

Love, to the ego, is like a business. It's always, somehow, a deal: I will give you this much love if you will meet these needs/requirements/fantasies of mine, and if you don't perform as I expect, I will take back my love . . . !

The ego thinks that love is a sport or a game. When considering romance, the ego asks: "Can I *get* him or her? Can I behave in such a way that I'll attract my target? Will I *win?*" Romantic love becomes a sport in which only the score matters, as the ego continues to enhance itself by collecting scalps.

But the ego has a disastrous way of becoming trapped by its own love game. It says: "Hmmmm, this person appears able to behave the way that I want them to in order to meet my needs. How shall I behave in order to attract them?" And the ego begins to subtly alter your personality in ways that you hope will make you appear to be the "perfect person" for the other. You like what they like. You laugh at their jokes. You eat what they eat, listen to their music, take up their hobbies.

And it works. They're hooked. But guess what? The other person's ego has been playing the same game! They've also been altering themselves to fit what they sensed to be *your* requirements for becoming attracted.

And of course, eventually you will both tire of pretending to be something you're not. Your real preferences and real personalities will naturally begin to assert themselves, to your mutual disillusionment. Now you are "no longer meeting my needs" or "not the person I fell in love with." You've fallen in love with what you wanted the other person to be, not with them as they actually are.

How many times have you heard a sadder but wiser friend confide: "I really thought that after we were married they'd change. I thought that if I loved them enough . . ." That really means: I thought they'd change into the imaginary person my ego wanted them to be; I wanted the power of my ego to manipulate them "for their own good." Ego-driven love is not true love.

The Heart of True Love

Does love transform? Does it heal? Does it make a person whole? Absolutely. Yes. Positively without a doubt. But the love that acts this way is love in its higher form: love that comes from the heart. Without conditions, without measure, without deals or tradeoffs. Love that accepts what it loves, lumps and all, just as it is.

This is the love that you feel for your children or parents. No matter how they may behave, they are still an integral part of your life. It's the love you may feel for a good friend. The choices that they make in their life don't matter; you don't have an agenda of your own for them. You only want them to be happy. And their happiness becomes your happiness.

Real love is compassionate. It has nothing to forgive because it expects nothing of what it loves. It accepts everything. It loves because love is its nature. This is the pure love of self-acceptance, the love that is always within you, waiting for recognition. Cultivating this higher form of love is a constant opportunity for personal growth, and a great benefit to both you and to those with whom you share this love.

It's right and good to be positively "self-centered." That means working from your inner core of compassionate love and wholeness. Nearly every great culture has had its own version of our Golden Rule: Love your neighbor *as yourself.* This reflects the profound human truth that you can't give what you haven't got, and it is in loving your own inner self that you learn to love others. Charity—or in the original Latin, *caritas,* meaning "compassionate love"—begins at home. And you can't be closer to home than when you are making room for your own human nature.

SELF-ACCEPTANCE GENERATES STRENGTH

Self-acceptance visibly changes the energy that you project outward to others, too. You change from weakness to strength. Your acceptance of yourself—and others—replaces an energy of resistance and negativity with the love and security that enable others to respond positively.

"I know what you mean," David, a prominent investment banker, told me. David had quit drinking two years earlier. "At first, I was very ambivalent about my inability to drink, especially because my clients are a bunch of party hearties. I wasn't sure they'd accept me anymore.

"But it's funny: once I'd accepted in my own heart that I wasn't drinking at our lunches, it became a kind of strength, you know? My clients would order mineral water for me without me saying anything, and no one joked about it or was embarrassed or anything."

David's self-acceptance allowed his clients to respond positively as well. When he wasn't fighting himself, neither did anyone else. Make no mistake: real love is a powerful force for change.

The Agony of Expectation

Although accepting parts of yourself sometimes feels painful or disappointing there's nothing wrong with you. You're not the problem. It's your expectations about yourself that create pain.

The gap between those expectations, ideas, masks, and false self-images and where you really are is an index of your psychic agony. It's like this: if you're driving your car along at fifty miles an hour and enjoying the trip, you're happy. But drive at fifty when you want to do sixty-five, and instead of fifty miles an hour of contentment, you have fifteen miles an hour of frustration.

It's okay to have expectations. We all have images of things as we'd like them to be and that's a necessary part of goal making and affirmation, which we'll talk about later. But don't fall in love with your dreams so much that you can't accept life as it unfolds toward those eventual goals.

When you're in pain about something in your life, you know that's a signal that your expectations are different than the actual outcome. Trust the outcome; let go of the expectations. It helps sometimes to downgrade those expectations to preferences, saying: "Well, I would have preferred. . . ." But don't weaken yourself by wasting energy on what isn't. You have more important things to deal with. Focus your energy on what is.

* * *

Freeing Up Your Energy

Using awareness in the present moment allows you to become focused on what you need to do right now. Using self-acceptance allows you to drop emotional burdens and side issues to free up your energy, both physical and emotional.

Inertia is not the lack of energy. It *is* energy, but energy that has been turned against itself, frozen, so to speak, by its own tangle of conflict and lack of a clear focus. It is energy that has been parceled out and mortgaged on a million unimportant things.

It is important to remember that life energy is a living thing; it is like a flow of current. As a metaphor for the life force the concept of electricity has certain limitations—but it can be useful in better understanding life energy. In this case, when we create anything with our minds—ideas, wants, needs, fears, hopes, issues, or conflicts—it is useful to think of the mind acting as a kind of "circuit designer" for the flow of our inner energy.

When we create an issue or stress in our minds, we are not simply spending energy on that issue on a one-time basis, but rather setting up a circuit that will continue to draw life energy "current" as long as we continue to believe in or worry about or think about that issue. No wonder we feel drained of energy and full of inertia at times. We are fighting with so many things in our mind that inner conflict continues to drain us. Self-acceptance allows you to drop these unnecessary energy drains.

Living with the Unforgivable

Accepting your actions and yourself may make terrific sense until you get to that one thing that has you saying: "But I just can't accept *that* about myself! It's unforgivable!" It *isn't* really unforgivable. But it's okay if you can't seem to forgive yourself; just let it be for now. At least, stop hating it, and yourself. Just leave it in neutral.

Your fear and dislike create a far bigger monster than you would actually have to deal with if you could see it clearly, with awareness and acceptance. Don't worry; you may find that by accepting the rest of yourself you'll create an energy of love and self-acceptance that is a powerful dissolver of "unacceptable" behavior.

"Will I Become a Happy Blob?"

Mark, a real estate agent, was afraid of something else: "If I accept myself as I am, and decide that I actually like myself, I'm afraid that I'll become so complacent I'll settle into a happy blob and never care about improving again. I'm afraid to be too contented!"

Mark's fear is natural. Most of us, if we have a dream of perfect, contented bliss somewhere, think that it should be anywhere but here, with our flabby muscles and two packs a day and too much awful dinner. Why should anybody be contented with *this?* We may think, sure, I could settle in here and be happy as I am, but what would happen to all my dreams and ambitions?

In a word, nothing. No matter how happy you decide to be right now, your own human nature will compel you to continually strive to meet your needs and goals in life. Those needs and goals—whether for accomplishment, love, friendship, money, power, creativity, spiritual growth, saving the whales, or just having fun—are in fact the reason you were born.

It's true. If you had nothing to do, nothing that you wanted or needed in this lifetime you wouldn't be here. You'd be free of all earthly encumbrances, a saint, liberated from all your karma, finished with your development and eternally blissful. The purpose of your life may truly be defined by those needs you feel, and your sense of purpose will evolve toward higher and higher goals as you grow. Your human nature will see to it that you continually move toward these goals, no matter how happy or sad you may feel at the time.

Whatever is important to you—if it's truly meaningful for you—won't vanish because you decide to accept and be happy with yourself right now.

Happiness in Small Doses

Self-acceptance, and the inner happiness that comes with it, is not an all-or-nothing phenomenon. It's something you can learn to do little by little. Every day there are as many opportunities to accept yourself just as you are right now as there are moments in the day.

The heiress who has her champagne luncheon for twelve, on a private terrace overlooking the Riviera, simply *ruined* because the roses aren't the right shade of pink is a source of head-shaking amusement to the rest of us. Yet we persist in saying: If only I were (a) fifteen pounds lighter, (b) earning an extra few thousand, (c) driving a newer car, *then* I could be happy. But not yet; not right now. Right now I've got to be miserable so that, someday, I can be happy. Well, it may be true that a little bit of pain makes the pleasures all that much sweeter, but who ever said you should focus on the pain all the time?

The Seeds of Inner Willpower

As you're beginning to understand something of what self-acceptance can mean for you, you might be starting to feel some of its subtle and far-reaching effects already, both in the way that your body feels after doing the Self-acceptance Experience, and in the feelings and attitudes toward yourself that may begin to evolve over the next few weeks or months.

You may experience a greater sense of personal security, a

sense of having somehow put yourself on firmer emotional ground. Or it may be reflected in a sense of greater personal comfort with your project, even a sense of humor about the state of your accomplishments with it. Life, somehow, may begin to seem more manageable. You can enhance this process by repeating the Self-acceptance Experience whenever you feel the need.

This inner confidence—it is actually the beginning of trust in your own inner life—is an important step forward in mastering your own inner willpower. You've found your true strength; it was there inside you all along. It's the strength of positivity, of trust, of loving yourself as you really are. It's the strength of life itself. And now it's working in your favor.

It will grow; you've planted the seeds.

8
Taking Action When You're Stuck

Now that you've become acquainted with the skills of awareness and self-acceptance, you're ready to take your willpower project in hand and learn about the third inner willpower skill: the art of conscious action.

Conscious Action Frees You

There is a wonderful moment of totality we sometimes experience when we are completely engrossed in the action of the present moment, fully aware of ourselves, our environment, and our activity. Perhaps we are walking along the seashore. Or humming a tune. Or making love, or jogging, or driving our car. We become one with our action. The action seems to carry itself along. We are no longer the doer, or merely the observer, yet we are in complete control. We are at peace with our activity. We are free.

In those moments, we can appreciate the words of W. B. Yeats:

> O body swayed to music, O brightening glance,
> How can we know the dancer
> from the dance?

This totality is one of the natural pleasures of life, a state of inner and outer harmony, unity and integration, that we seek as our birthright. But because we don't always understand what brings this state of totality about, we frequently waste large amounts of time waiting for some elusive "it" to happen before we begin to act. In fact, this state of totality is the result of action; it doesn't precede it.

The First Law of Willpower Action

Fred, back at his office, was frustrated in his exercise program for this reason. "I was doing really well for a while, working out three nights a week. Then I got busy at the office and had to skip a few weeks, and I don't know exactly what happened: I just couldn't get back into it. I was out of sync somehow. I kept waiting for the right time to get back into it, but I'm still waiting—I'm not sure for what. . . ."

Fred's dilemma brings us to what we might call the First Law of Willpower Action:

> There is no such thing as the "right" time,
> only the present time.

No moment is ever completely without its favorable and unfavorable influences. That's life. Ask any good astrologer—whose profession it is to discern whether the astral influences for any moment are "good" or "bad" or "so-so"—about the right time for anything. They'll respond by rolling their eyes skyward and muttering something about "It depends. . . ."

The present time can be made into the perfect time. No matter what else is happening, the biggest influence on any moment is your activity. You mold the present moment with your actions. It is your choices and your actions that create the totality of the perfect moment for you.

You achieve totality with your actions by setting out to do it.

Achieving this totality is something that you are learning how to create by using your skills of inner willpower. By becoming focused on your breathing, by choosing to enter the present moment more fully, by integrating and centering your energies, you are setting into motion a process that yields totality and freedom as its outcome.

This means that waiting for "the right time" to act is futile. Instead, the only time you'll ever have to work with is the present. And the present time is as good as any for action.

By using your inner willpower skills you've learned how to act from a new location in your life: from the stronger, more secure place of being fully where you are, right now.

You are in touch with the source of your inner willpower. And you know how to reach it whenever you wish. You don't need to wait for totality.

The Second Law of Willpower Action

The Second Law of Willpower Action is:

Just do it anyway.

It's okay to be unready, imperfect, not in the mood, or half-baked about something to do it anyway. You don't have to feel totally enthusiastic, convinced, virtuous, or even awake in order to choose to act in the direction of your willpower project or in favor of anything else you want to do. You merely have to focus on your next task and set your body in motion, first of all with your breathing, and then in whatever way is necessary. The enthusiasm and the commitment will follow.

Sometimes it's simply a case of: deliver your body to the gym, or to the health food store, or to your desk and sit down. Just get it there. It doesn't matter how you feel about it, or whether you think you're doing a very good job of it.

DON'T FEELINGS COME FIRST?

Why, you might reasonably ask, are you now saying that my internal state doesn't matter when you've just spent so much time showing me how to change it at will?

One of the wonderful things about the relationship between the mind and the body is this: not only does the state of mind directly influence the body but the reverse is also true. The state of the body directly influences the mind! This is one of the ancient, long-proven principles of yoga. And it is why the simple act of relaxed breathing can have such a profound effect on your inner state. You can use the body to integrate the mind, or the mind to harmonize the body.

Action of any kind in the direction of your willpower project will actually help to activate your inner willpower, even if you don't "feel like it." Whenever you change your physical posture or position, your inner state automatically shifts to align with your body's new state. Researchers in neurolinguistic programming, or NLP, have shown how some depressed people can rapidly improve their mood simply by changing their posture from a "depressed" mode—eyes down, shoulders drooping, breathing shallow—to a "happy" mode—eyes lifted, shoulders back, chest wide.

The simple act of smiling has been shown time and again to produce feelings of well-being, sociability, and optimism. Anthony Robbins, author of the excellent *Unlimited Power,* notes that it is almost impossible for someone to continue weeping in distress if you ask them to look up. The crying stops as soon as they lift their eyes.

You may remember the old Rodgers and Hammerstein song about "Whenever I feel afraid, I whistle a happy tune . . . and I always fool myself as well." That's exactly what faking it will actually do for you. Even when you haven't got it together, acting as if you do will be followed by the inner confidence and strength just as though you meant it all along. The following experience clearly demonstrates how your body influences your mind.

Inner Willpower Experience No. 7: The Body Shift

If you're sitting comfortably or lying down as you read this, allow yourself to slump down into your chair a few more inches. Slide down a bit so you're resting on your lower spine.

Allow your chest to cave in naturally. Let it go.

Let your feet and legs go limp. Just let them flop. Feel how your breathing has changed. Is it faster or slower? Deeper or more shallow? Is there lightness or heaviness?

Now pretend and heave a deep, slow miserable sigh. Make a sad, pitiful sound as the air leaves your body. Go for an Academy Award.

What is happening to your face? What can you feel about the expression you're wearing? Where are your eyebrows? Is there stress between them? Are your eyelids drooping in woe? Is your mouth sagging at the corners? What can you taste inside your mouth: sweetness or bitterness?

How do you feel? What's happened to your energy? Where did all these troubles come from in twenty seconds? How has your awareness changed?

We can't leave you like this. Take a deep breath and sit upright, so that your spine is naturally straight and comfortable and you are not resting against anything. Place your feet on the floor. Sit so that you are seated on your bottom, not your spine. Breathe naturally.

* * *

Relax and make any adjustments to your posture so that you are seated comfortably erect, almost as though you were standing.

Now relax, and allow your upper body to come into natural alignment by floating forward or backward just slightly. Let your trunk come to rest at the comfortable, natural center of balance, resting lightly above your hips.

Let go of your shoulders and arms. Let them drop. Release your fingers. Let them go. Feel how much habitual tension you've suddenly dropped, just by letting it go.

Take a deep, free breath and allow your chest to open and lift upward naturally. Feel how much lighter your body feels.

Glance upward, toward the top of a door or window. Continue to breathe comfortably, allowing your head to float upward, following your gaze. Look into the distance beyond where you are seated now. Remain here for a few moments.

Go ahead: put down this book and try it.

What are you experiencing? How has your energy shifted? What is your mood now?

Let's take this one step further: How would you sit right now if you were perfectly self-confident and completely in command of yourself? What would it look and feel like? How would you change your posture from the inside? Just pretend. Imagine what it feels like. If you prefer, pretend to be perfectly successful and happy, on top of the world. What would your posture, facial expression, and breathing feel like?

Allow any subtle shifts to your posture or breathing that begin to happen as you pretend to be what you've chosen. Just go ahead; let your body move in any way that it wishes. Allow any gestures or nuances to express themselves. *Be* confident and successful.

You'll find it easier to experiment with your body position if you put this book down, experiment with your posture for a few moments, and then continue following this experience.

Observe how your posture and breathing have shifted subtly. What does your breathing feel like? Notice where the breath energy is going inside your body. What parts is it reaching?

What expression is on your face? What subtle changes have happened?

What's happening in the center of your body: Is it tighter or more relaxed? Lighter or more solid? Just feel it.

Are you relaxed, or tense? Become aware of the subtle balance of energy, of how deeply rooted in relaxation you can be and still be alert and effective.

Remain aware. Just let your body and breathing flow naturally. Take your time. Enjoy this.

Are you smiling? What's your energy like? Who's in charge now?

What have you become aware of about your posture or breathing that will be useful to you in everyday life? What changes can be helpful? Remind yourself how easily you can now enter your chosen state.

Now think of something you've been meaning to do. Put down this book and go do it. Have a glance in the mirror while you're at it to see how you look right now, when you're feeling confident and in charge of your actions.

100 Proof Synthetic Willpower

This little experience has mind-boggling implications for your well-being and happiness. You can bring your mind and inner state right to where you want it, just by shifting your body. You can *be* confident and purposeful simply by acting "as though" you are confident and purposeful.

It is possible to achieve inner and outer balance by starting with the body, by starting from action and letting the feelings follow. The body is a powerful tool.

The best way to use the power of The Body Shift to strengthen your inner willpower is by acting "as if" whenever you feel the need for some extra willpower. You may want to think of the experiences below as synthetic willpower, but they work just as well as the real thing. And results are what matters. Synthetic willpower can be very handy, especially when you're stuck on your inner willpower project.

Synthetic Willpower No. 1: Acting As If

Use your breathing to enter the present moment. Bring yourself fully here.

Ask yourself: How would I look right now if I had perfect inner willpower? How would I stand? How would I move? How would I breathe? What would my body feel like?

Allow yourself to begin to feel whatever you are imagining. Just let yourself improvise. Make any changes necessary to your posture or your breathing.

* * *

If you aren't sure what inner willpower would feel like, imagine yourself to be in perfect command of yourself, relaxed and completely comfortable with your situation, able to act with complete freedom and harmony.

Imagine that each incoming breath is bringing you greater personal power, in the form of a glowing golden light.

Ask: If I had perfect willpower right now, what would I say? What would I do? How would I feel?

And just pretend: stand, move, breathe, and act as you would if you could do exactly what you choose. Be bold. Have fun.

You might like to experiment with this variation:

Synthetic Willpower No. 2: The Pillar of Power

At first, this is easiest to do if you are standing up. Later, you can do this while sitting down.

Take a deep, slow breath in the present moment.

Imagine that you are completely enclosed by a glowing pillar of golden light that extends from the core of the earth, through your body, to the heavens. This pillar of energy comfortably surrounds and protects your body, extending out around it. Just imagine it, either with your eyes open or closed, or simply "sense" that this pillar of light is here now.

Begin to breathe in the secure, glowing energy of this pillar. With each incoming breath, allow it to permeate every cell of your body. As you breathe, imagine the energy of the pillar is becoming stronger and stronger: perhaps it glows more brightly, or becomes larger or more dense. Follow your imagination.

Feel, or sense, the energy of this pillar of strength as it extends downward through the soles of your feet and upward through your body, out the top of your head. Feel its stability, its protective strength, its goodness penetrating throughout your body. See how the energy of this pillar of light insulates you from all negativity and fear.

Continue breathing consciously and naturally. Allow your body to stretch and move freely into harmony with this pillar of power. Allow any subtle shifts of weight or balance or muscle tone to express themselves. Take your time; experience this moment fully.

How are you standing? Where are your shoulders? Your head? Your back and spine? How are you breathing? How do you feel? Become aware.

Allow this pillar of energy to move with you and accompany you for as long as you wish.

Act and move as though you have perfect inner willpower.

The Third Law of Willpower Action

The least that you need to do
is all that you need to do

The only action you can ever really do is in the present moment, which is this moment that is rolling along with you. Each moment makes relatively small demands on you. The more that you can focus your awareness on what's right in front of you this instant, and on what you need to do right here and now, the smaller that action needs to be.

Action in the present moment is just the small motion your body needs to do to carry you forward in your task. It could mean just standing up, or heading toward the door, or picking up the next memo, or reaching for the chewing gum instead of the cigarette. Action becomes only what you need to do within the space of a single breath. It's never going to be more than you can handle.

Action Is Simple

Think of using your inner willpower as you would a martial arts skill if you were a judo or tae qwon do master. That is, you need only use the inner force necessary to shift the balance in your favor. You need only do the action that is appropriate right now. Just enough, no more. The masterful use of inner willpower lies in doing only what is necessary at this moment. You don't need a nuclear blast to swat a fly.

Action is simple. It's merely turning away from the deli counter, or smiling at someone, or changing the subject, or putting on your running shoes. One step at a time. That's all.

Action in the present can simply mean sitting and breathing when necessary. Action can sometimes mean a deliberate choice not to respond to an otherwise perfectly reasonable temptation or provocation. Focus on finding the positive action that you can do right now. It's a much faster way to strengthen your inner willpower—and eventually, your "won't power," too.

Look for the Light

Focusing on something positive is one of the most potent ways to strengthen your inner willpower. This means not wasting time or energy thinking about what you can't do or won't do, or habits you are trying to avoid or drop. Instead, focus on what you can or will do, even if all you can do at that moment is simply reach for some veggies or look out the window or head for the door. It's much more effective than dwelling on what you won't do, and far less agonizing.

Someone once asked my yoga master, Yogi Amrit Desai, how to drop bad habits. Yogi Desai responded by asking a question in return: If you come into a room that is full of darkness, how do you get rid of the dark? The young man who had asked him pondered for a minute, then replied hesitantly: Turn on the light? Yogi Desai smiled. And now where, he asked further, has the darkness gone? The young man seemed overwhelmed by the metaphysical improbabilities posed by this second question.

Yogi Desai laughed genially. Does it really matter? he asked, gently. Turning on the light solved the problem. When you wish to get rid of darkness you don't try to push it away, argue with it, struggle with it, or reason with it. You simply bring in some light. Where the darkness "goes" isn't relevant.

It is the same, my yoga master continued, with darkness in your life. Focus on what you are doing to bring yourself light. Let bad habits take care of themselves. Be positive.

The Cure for Inertia

What about those times when you feel trapped in inertia and immobility? What can you do when your inner willpower project seems like the Ironman Triathalon as viewed from a sickbed?

The same law of minimum action applies here, too. When you're stuck, physical action of any kind will shift the balance from inner inertia to outer activity.

There's an old trick that horsemen use when a horse freezes and balks at the prospect of wading into a swiftly moving stream. Instead of futilely urging the horse forward into the water and meeting every ounce of resistance that a half-ton of muscle can offer, the horseman will simply turn the horse's head aside, as though turning away from the stream. He'll urge the horse to walk in a circle. Once the horse's muscles have unlocked and he's moving again, the horseman will simply walk him into the stream sideways. Same trick works for us humans, too. When you're stuck, just start moving—in any direction!

This brings us to the Finger Wiggle Trick, a quick way to unlock your ability to act.

The Finger Wiggle Trick

Next time you feel trapped, inert, and frustrated, and keep running through your mind that you're "supposed to be" adding another page to your novel or doing five sit-ups or folding the laundry, and all you can do is sit on the sofa, do this:

Take a slow, relaxed breath and become aware of your body, just sitting where you are. Feel where your arms are, your legs, your back, and chest. Feel yourself sitting.

Focus on your fingers, or your toes. Begin to do the very least action that you can do right now: wiggle them. Move your fingers or toes in any way at all. Just wiggle. Feel how this simple movement is beginning to increase your heart rate and deepen your breathing.

Allow the movement to extend into your hand: clench your fist open and closed. Or wiggle and bounce your entire foot and extend the motion into your lower leg.

Now involve your whole arm: stretch and move it in any way that feels good. Extend the movement into your body. Or extend the movement of your legs into a standing position. That's it! Stand up and move around. Breathe deeply.

Remind yourself of what you wanted to do. Ask yourself: What's the smallest action I need to do *now?* And do it.

9

Body Willpower: What It Is and How It Works

David, the investment banker, eyed me keenly. "I can understand how awareness and self-acceptance might improve my internal focus and give me a kind of inner strength. But why do I need to work with my body to improve my willpower?"

The reason you need to work with your body is because your willpower actually has a physical center in your body, a locale whose power and efficiency can actually be improved with proper exercise and care. You can actually strengthen your body's ability to easily carry out your wishes by paying attention to this center.

Your physical center of willpower is called the *hara.* Yoga calls it the *tanden;* sufi schools, the *kath;* and western medicine, the *solar plexus.* You might know it as the pit of your stomach. It's where your "gut feelings" are located.

FINDING YOUR INNER WILLPOWER CENTER

The hara is easy to locate. You know the spot instinctively. It's that place that twists or tightens or gets queasy when there's something not right in your surroundings or feelings. It's the place that goes Uh-oh. It's the place that feels warm and cozy when you hug a baby or curl up with a favorite book.

If you can't quite put your finger on it, imagine this: a fist is about to punch you suddenly in the abdomen. It's the spot you would instinctively reach down and double over to protect. It is just below your belly button and deep inside. The very thought of being punched makes it tighten, doesn't it? You've just located your hara.

The hara is a large and very sensitive nerve plexus that physiologists consider a kind of subbrain, the center of your autonomic nervous system. It is the hara, and not the brain, that actually operates your breathing, heart rate, and other "automatic" motor functions.

But the hara is much more than just a nerve plexus. It is also a living bioelectric energy field, a battery that draws and stores energy from its environment. The hara is the primary interchange for energies within your body, and between your body and its environment.

It is as this energy interchanges that the hara becomes the physical center of your willpower. As such, the hara is the seat of your strength, the storehouse of your vitality and lifeforce.

A Strong Hara Means Strong Willpower

A strong, well-functioning hara gives strength and stamina, both physically and emotionally. It grants you independence from outside disturbances—paradoxically because its energy interchange capabilities plug you in more strongly to the energy of your environment, reducing the friction between you and your circumstances and enabling you to respond more spontaneously and appropriately to life around you.

A strong hara gives you a sense of natural balance, both physically and emotionally, that allows you to remain composed and in command of yourself under even the most difficult circumstances.

A well-functioning hara gives you a kind of center of gravity, an energy that causes others to describe such a person as "substantial" or "solid." The person with a strong hara is quietly confident and secure. Hara gives your body a sense of physical freedom, of natural movement and posture that enables you to use your energy field with maximum efficiency.

Your Body's Telecommunications System

We've been talking about the hara as a key component of the body's energy field. This energy field is not simply fashionable hocus pocus. It's real. Some of the newest discoveries of contemporary medicine are brilliantly illuminating traditional teachings of the most ancient oriental and Indian masters about this aspect of the body.

Medical science has devised something called the magnetoencephalographic scan, the MEG, a device that picks up extremely subtle electrical activity in the living brain and translates the amount of activity into different colors on a map of the brain. Before the invention of MEG, scientists could not actually observe the living brain in operation; they could only dissect a dead one. Dissection showed nerves and ganglia—the wiring, as it were—but it could never show what the wiring did when it was in operation.

With MEG, they discovered that the living brain creates a kind of electrical field around itself, and that it is changes in the level of this field, not impulses along nerve "wires," that determine the state of the brain's activity.

The brain, for all practical purposes, engages in bioelectric telecommunications. The body is not merely a hard-wired set of cables, but communicates and relates to itself via methods more analogous to the properties of light, sound, or electricity. These discoveries are even now being expanded into research on the body's bioelectric field as a whole.

Scientists have only begun addressing what ancient civilizations have long taught: that this bioelectric field of the body is interactive—it is capable of absorbing and utilizing extremely subtle and sophisticated energies from the natural fields of the earth and the atmosphere, and of affecting these fields as well. Scientists are only beginning to grapple with this concept; we don't yet have instruments of sufficient sensitivity to measure these fields.

But that doesn't prevent us from making practical use of ancient knowledge. You don't have to be able to explain everything scientifically in order to use it on a practical basis. We can use electricity, or even the force of gravity in a practical way without understanding everything about "why" it works the way it does.

It's the same thing with the force fields of the body. They work. They have natural laws. They can be harnessed, like the wind or the tide or the flame, to work for your benefit.

Harnessing Your Body's Energy

The hara's capacity to process and use the energy around you and within you for your benefit improves considerably with exercise. Not simply physical exercise—although that's certainly beneficial—but a more subtle form of exercise that coordinates and harmonizes your physical, mental, and emotional states.

It's an exercise that takes maximum advantage of the body's natural energy circuits and regenerative capabilities. It's an exercise that for many centuries was taught secretly only to the highest adepts of the oriental martial arts and within Tibetan monasteries. It's what gave legendary strength and speed to oriental warriors, and the skill of *tumo*—the near-miraculous ability of Tibetan monks to sit naked in a snowstorm wrapped in a wet sheet without freezing, drying the sheet with the body heat they generate from their strong hara.

The secret exercise is hara breathing. Yes, breathing. This profound link between you and your environment has its nexus point, not in your lungs, but in your hara. True, the lungs exchange the air. But the air acts only as a kind of carrier for a process of energy exchange that is completed deep within the body, within the hara. The full cycle of breathing, properly done, completes a vital energy circuit within the body.

THE SECRETS OF HARA BREATHING

Thus far, in our series of Inner Willpower Experiences, we've focused on the incoming breath primarily as a way to bring new energy into the body. And we've used the outgoing breath mostly as a vehicle for letting go of old tensions and stale energies. With hara breathing, we'll look at what happens with the tail end of that outgoing breath: the bottom of the breath, not just the part that is expelled by the diaphragm from the lungs, but the last part that's released with a subtle contraction of the belly and upper abdomen.

Inner Willpower Experience No. 8: Hara Breathing

Take your next ordinary inward breath and let it exhale naturally, without changing anything. When you get to the bottom of this breath, continue breathing outward by contracting your belly just slightly, to release an extra bit of energy. It's like a slight "push" upward. Or whisper the sound of "hah" as you get to the bottom. Allow the last bit of air to make a breathy, airy sound.

Do not hold at the bottom. Simply allow your attention to focus on this part of your belly that contracts naturally.

Release the belly easily and allow the inward breath to follow naturally, without interruption or holding at the top.

Expel this second breath with a slow, natural exhalation, and again focus on your hara as the last bit leaves the bottom with a slight contraction or the sound of "hah." Be gentle; do not force.

Breathe in a third time. Your lungs and belly may fill more deeply this time; just allow them to respond naturally.

As you breathe outward, focus on your hara and become aware of any changes in sensation you may feel in that part of your body. Does it seem somehow slightly warmer—or cooler? Does it seem smaller—or larger? Does it seem to have a color, or sound? Simply notice how it seems and become aware of your hara as you continue to focus on the last part of your outgoing breath.

After a half-dozen such hara breaths, many people begin to experience a sensation of subtle warmth in the hara region. To some, it may even seem to be a glowing ball of energy. Others may notice that the air itself seems to be somehow heavier or richer, or that the process of breathing seems to be activating itself into a deeper, more complete cycle.

Continue to focus on expelling the last bit of air from the hara.

What Hara Breathing Does for You

This deceptively simple exercise has a profound cleansing, harmonizing, and energizing effect on your entire body. It is activating and strengthening your hara and the deeper circuits of your body with every single exhalation. Hara breathing purifies and balances subtle neurochemical energy fields, which will release deeply held energy blockages and improve your strength, stamina, and even mental clarity—because your brain is the direct beneficiary of better energy balance.

Hara breathing isn't an "instant fix," however. It's something that you can continue to gain increasing benefits from in the weeks and months ahead, as long as you pay attention to allowing the expulsion of that extra bit of air, even if only for a few moments every day.

The benefits of hara breathing begin to show themselves, not in your body, but in other areas of your life: in the way you don't get rattled as easily when the traffic is slow, or when your flight is canceled. In the way you can stick it out at your desk or at your project for a few minutes longer. In the way that someone else's bad mood rolls off of you, instead of bugging you. In the way that you begin to sleep more soundly, or exercise more easily, or eat more confidently.

Hara is subtle; its beneficial effects often show up only in hindsight, when you realize that you "haven't done that" in quite some time. Or when your friends say: "You look really good! What have you been doing?"

No Flat Stomachs, Please

The great temptation with hara breathing is to think that we can short-circuit or speed up the process by doing abdominal strengthening exercises: sit-ups, or sucking in the gut. We mistake the concept of a "flat abdomen" for that of a "strong belly."

You will be pleased to know that a strong hara most emphatically has nothing to do with a flat stomach. Flat stomachs are for children and teenagers, who know nothing about real stamina to begin with. In order to strengthen and develop the hara properly, you must release the belly to allow a complete, natural cycle of inward and outward breathing. You've got to allow the center of your body to breathe and respond freely.

Holding in your stomach has absolutely nothing to do with developing your inner—or outer—strength. In fact, it is actually detrimental to it, forcing your body to breathe only from the rib cage and shoulders, cutting off half of the energy circuit. The old military posture of "chest out, stomach in" actually weakens you. If you really needed your strength for a physical contest, you'd instinctively crouch forward, and begin breathing from deep within. Your body knows this; don't let your mind tell it otherwise.

The Hara and Stress-Proofing

The hara has another interesting property: it's the direct link between your emotions and your body. It's what absorbs stress. It's also where healing, soothing energies are most effectively used.

If you think for a moment of a healing, soothing warmth surrounding you—a protective, snuggly, secure energy—where does it instinctively do you the most good? Where do you want to absorb it in order to feel better? In your shoulders? Your legs? Your head? Or deep into your belly?

Draw this friendly energy into your hara right now and see. Just imagine a soft light being drawn directly into your midsection as you breathe in. What do you feel of your body's response?

In the hara, the energy quickly relaxes you, warms you, allows you to feel secure. You may even notice that your breathing has just changed. Perhaps your belly is rising and falling slowly, in a more relaxed and easy fashion. Maybe something indescribable has let go. That's your hara's spontaneous and natural reaction to good energy: energy that you can create and draw on simply by thinking about it.

The hara acts as a useful and infallible gauge of your emotions and general level of comfort or discomfort. When you're happy and relaxed and secure, it sort of "opens" like the pupil of your eye to allow your physical energy to flow freely. Any threat to your well-being, or negative energy, causes it to tighten and close to protect your body's circuits from harmful energies.

The hara doesn't have any "brains" in the conventional sense, but it knows what it likes. Its mission is to seek out and maintain harmonious energies for your body, so it constantly monitors the energy of both your body and your environment, responding and adapting to changes. Because the hara doesn't "think" like a brain, it can't be fooled or swayed by your mind's arguments one way or another. It just knows that something is causing you an imbalance, and it doesn't like that. It won't accept rationalizations.

This straightforward quality of the hara makes it eminently useful as a gauge of what's right for you and what isn't. It'll tell you when you're on the right track in your life.

When you tell yourself something and it's the truth—that is, when it lines up with the greater order and harmony of the universe—your hara smiles and relaxes and you feel good all over. The center of your body feels comfortable and easy. The emotional juices might be flowing, but it feels right and okay. But a rationalization or a bad situation? It lurches, somehow. Or sits like a lump. It's your body saying "I can't swallow that one!"

If you seek hara comfort in all that you do, you can begin to eliminate many harmful elements from your life and replace them with beneficial, positive activities. Your hara will constantly alert you to potential harm if you listen to it. And it will respond gratefully to the good, healthful things that you do for yourself.

Your body is your best and most faithful friend. It will never lie to you. You can learn to ignore or override its messages or teach your body some very distorted habits, but left to its own natural devices, your body is totally honest. And that honesty can become a powerful ally of your best interests and your inner willpower.

Follow your breath out, now.

Use it to strengthen your inner willpower.

10
Taking a Self-Protective Approach to Discipline

"What I need is some discipline. I guess it would be good for me."

Samantha shuddered as though she had just bitten into a lemon. The very thought was horrible, painful.

"That's what discipline is all about, isn't it: no pain, no gain?"

Actually, no.

Discipline is about structure—those support systems, schedules, limits, and encouragements that you put into place for yourself in order to help you do the things you choose. Real discipline is a carefully chosen set of actions or limits that provides a support for your priorities. Such disciplines, or practices, allow your better self to grow without being crushed by old habits and attitudes. A sense of personal discipline is one of the natural outcomes of your growing inner willpower.

Discipline Channels Your Energy

True discipline doesn't restrict or inhibit your energy. It merely channels the energy and focuses it along routes that you've chosen. Discipline is structure. It's like banks for a powerful river. Without the limitations of the banks, a mighty river would soon run riot, flooding the surrounding countryside, dissipating itself over a wide area and quickly ceasing to be a powerful or useful river. The banks are actually a kind of protection for the river's energy and identity.

Discipline supports you. Its limits and programs can provide your growing new self with some very important protection in the early days. A crib may be a restraining discipline for a baby, but it also protects the toddler from many, many household hazards until the child develops internal controls.

It might help to think about the improvements you want to make in your life as though they were a newborn baby or a tiny puppy: in need of careful shielding from all the potential trouble they can get into in the larger world you live in.

Eventually your sense of discipline will become internal and you'll naturally prefer to do the good things you've chosen for yourself. But for right now, you need the protection of a regular schedule, or a limited menu, or shopping only with cash not credit cards. Disciplines offer you positive guidelines and good habits for your new self. You need to set intelligent limits and pay attention to supporting your new behavior.

Your Comfort Zone

Disciplines can serve as a kind of boundary, or outer border, of your personal "comfort zone": that area of behavior with which you feel the most centered, balanced, and harmonious, that area that truly is the "real you."

Your true comfort zone may not lie where you think it does right now. It may not be merely a rough description of your present way of life. You may instead actually feel much better, be happier and more energetic by living within some new guidelines, like more exercise or less sugar, more time spent with family and friends, or less spent on shopping sprees. But you won't know that unless you try it, and unless you give yourself a fair chance to make it work.

Discipline Is Not Masochism

Discipline has nothing to do with self-inflicted pain or punishment. That's masochism. Or a guilt trip. Discipline has everything to do with choosing to work toward something from love, not from self-hatred and flagellation.

True discipline contains inherent rewards for you: perhaps better health or better looks, more personal energy, peace of mind, self-confidence or those tangible accomplishments that will carry you toward your goals and dreams. Discipline always has a good reason for you, a reward that far exceeds the effort you put into it. It may not seem that way at the outset, when discipline may look very much like deprivation, but in the long run the pursuit of what you love can make even extraordinary tradeoffs of discipline seem effortless.

The phenomenal personal discipline of a top Olympic athlete, for instance, is something that leaves the rest of us in awe: the seven-days-a-week training sessions, the predawn workouts, the carefully chosen diet, the limited social life, and the endless repetition of the basics of their sport are an awesome demonstration of total personal commitment to a goal.

And yet, if you ask athletes about discipline, they'll most likely shrug modestly and talk instead about how much they love their sport. Even Margaret Thatcher was once asked about the horrific demands that being England's Prime Minister placed on her. She responded without hesitation: "But I *love* this job!"

Discipline must follow what you love, not punish what you despise. That way, getting up a little earlier, or staying a little later, or cutting back, or letting go of a habit isn't something to groan about. It becomes simple when the action supports something you really want to do.

When Discipline Hurts

When discipline hurts it is because we've chosen inappropriate and excessive personal disciplines, and they're no better than shoes that don't fit us. They pinch and blister at every step. We soon stop using them and sigh in relief. Usually, we've chosen inappropriate disciplines because we really *expect* them to hurt. No wonder we soon end up metaphorically barefoot, our lives and our priorities without the simplest support and protection.

At the same time, it can't honestly be said that disciplines are fun every single minute—but are you really sure you're having constant fun with your bad habits right now? On balance, there's probably a lot of negative energy attached to those habits, or you wouldn't be feeling the need to get rid of them. Until a new discipline becomes a natural part of your life, it might be viewed as choosing to make some tradeoffs of short-term discomfort for long-term gain. It's much better to choose your own form of temporary discomfort, with real freedom waiting at the end of the journey, than to have increasing misery thrust upon you by a bad habit that holds only sickness, pain, and loss at the end of its road.

Discipline does *not* have to hurt in order to be effective. But it must be appropriate and supportive of you in your present circumstances. Each individual discipline or supporting practice must be something that you've chosen to use as a tool for your inner growth.

Disciplines Are Simple

A discipline focuses on one simple, specific thing. It isn't a blanket prescription, like: "I've got to do something about my tardiness" or "I've got to lose ten pounds." Discipline says what you specifically will do, instead. It says: "I'll leave twenty minutes earlier" or "I'll walk instead of drive."

Individual disciplines can be very simple, like choosing to set aside a certain time of day for your personal health or relaxation time, or returning-phone-calls-time, or children's story time. Or expanding the kinds of foods you eat to include a daily serving of something nutritious. Or having regular coffee only at breakfast, and decaf later in the day.

It may help to think of disciplines as guidelines for your behavior rather than as rigid rules. The concept of guidelines has some flexibility implied—you can do it later, or make an adjustment—that spares you the spasms of guilt and self-hatred that can come up when you don't live up to your own expectations for yourself, when you've opted out of your own answers.

Deepening Your Discipline

Discipline is built, not inflicted. Each discipline, each choice, is undertaken one at a time, gradually, experimentally, as part of a long-term program, not dumped on you all at once as an impossible list of demands and commands to yourself that set you up for failure before you've even begun.

If this description of choosing a suitable discipline sounds very much like something we discussed earlier—your project—you're right. Learning how to use personal discipline appropriately is very much a part of your inner willpower project. If you're wondering what sort of disciplines might be appropriate for you right now, your project is the place to look.

What have you already chosen to work on? What accomplishment concerning your project are you proudest of? What do you need to work on the most? What do you need to adjust? What area are you ready to expand or deepen? Do you want to go back and start over, rethinking your project entirely? It's up to you, but it's important to assess what you are doing for your project as well as what your project is doing for you.

YOUR COMMITMENT TO YOU

It's also important to be gentle with yourself in the patient, persistent application of your personal guidelines, without being a pushover. The choice of any individual discipline represents a commitment you've made to yourself to pursue one course of action over another in order to support your personal growth. Following that guideline can be a means of expressing your respect and love for the person you are becoming, for the newer, better you.

Commitment comes gradually. It grows from your experience, over time, over distance. It comes from love of what you want to achieve, and from a growing confidence in your ability to do it. It comes from understanding what you are dealing with, and a willingness to accept obstacles as part of the terrain. It comes from the growing certainty that what you value in life *is* important, meaningful, and worthy of your commitment.

Commitment to your daily practices themselves, to your personal disciplines and habits, to using the tools you have in hand to achieve those goals, is also gained gradually. It comes from seeing and feeling the good results of your discipline.

Commitment itself is a tool for your inner willpower. Making a short-term commitment—say ten weeks—to the daily practice of any new discipline will give you a solid basis of practical experience from which to make any adjustments and further, longer commitments. You'll be able to gain meaningful experience responding to a range of ordinary—and perhaps even extraordinary—obstacles. With a ten-week commitment you can set new habit patterns in motion and allow them to become a part of your life without the endless dither of waking up each morning wondering: Should I? After ten weeks, you'll be able to answer the question with authority based on your own practical experience.

Discipline ultimately simplifies your life. It allows you to live with intelligently chosen and practical answers, rather than being forced to reinvent your life every day with the endless question of: What should I do?

Cutting Down or Cutting Out?

Is it better discipline to cut back gradually or to simply go cold turkey? That depends.

For some people, gradually cutting back or building up a new habit allows them to maintain their inner equilibrium and stay within their comfort zone.

Margaret found that she made better progress cutting down her cholesterol intake by starting with the "easy" items first.

"I used to have eggs for breakfast all the time without thinking about it. But I don't care about them all that much, so now I just have them once in a while.

"But hamburgers! I'd die if I thought I could never have another. So I have them, and enjoy them. Right now it's easier for me to stop putting butter on my bread as a next step. I think the burgers and fries will be the last to go!"

Margaret had learned how to do what was possible for her, gradually shifting her dietary habits in a way that was comfortable for her. She was wisely refraining from tackling her major personal challenges until she had developed sufficient inner willpower to feel comfortable doing so.

The "No" Solution

Does this mean that "trying to cut down" on something is an easier and more appropriate discipline than simply saying "No"? Not by a long shot. Saying no can be far easier on your psyche than the endless, pointless flirtation with disaster that having "maybe just a little" can provoke. Sometimes you just don't need the aggravation.

The ability to say "No, I can't handle that right now" comes from a real respect for your inner abilities, and a strong desire to give yourself a chance to grow in a positive way. Saying "no" is a loving and generous thing to do for yourself, a real boundary of protection that is far wiser than exposing yourself to the unnecessary hazards of whatever you are choosing to avoid.

Chloe, the owner of a small boutique, saw very clearly that anything creamy was her downfall. "I could pass up snacks, salty things, extra portions. Everything. But put a pint of ice cream or some yogurt in front of me and I was out of control. I couldn't have just a scoop; I'd eat the whole pint—and then another, and more.

"I had to accept that for right now, dairy things are off the menu for me. I can't handle them. They're like an allergy; they put me right out of control. Right now, there's no such thing as 'just a taste' for me. And it's much, much easier this way."

The Secrets of "Won't Power"

There's a secret to saying no and making it your easiest escape:

The first "no" is the easiest.

The sooner you say it, and the further away from the actual temptation you are, the stronger and easier it becomes. But that means that the "no" must be said immediately and strongly to your own mind at the first glimmering of temptation, to your own thoughts, before it is spoken externally.

If you can nip the thought in the bud, by saying no *and turning your mind toward something else,* your external behavior will follow right along.

But if you've ever sat and thought about "just a taste" of a favorite but off-the-menu food, or a cigarette or drink or pastime, you know that saying the "no" is not the problem. The problem is in stopping your thoughts from continuing to dangle what you don't want in front of your overheated imagination.

Merely trying "not to think of" something is an insoluble bind. Ancient yogic masters used to give this problem as a lesson in supreme mental skill:

The Elephant Conundrum

For the next ten seconds, try *not* to think of an elephant. Just close your eyes and don't think about elephants.

Funny, there's elephants hopping all over the page now, aren't there? When was the last time you thought about them otherwise? The lesson here is that telling your brain *not* to do something only turns it right into the direction of whatever you're trying to avoid.

Your brain simply isn't programmed *not to do* whatever. Trying not to think of something, or telling yourself to do something in the negative, like "Don't fall," requires a complicated linguistic translation for your brain from the negative "Don't fall" command into: "Oh yeah, what he means is: walk carefully." Making that translation requires your brain to have a ready positive alternative at hand, otherwise it may end up saying: "Fall? Fall? Trip? Stumble? . . . Oooops!" And away you go.

What *is* effective for thought-stopping is simply to redirect the mind toward something else by distracting it with another activity. The mind prefers to be constantly active, to be constantly paying attention to something, and indeed, to anything at all. That's your leverage: when temptation appears, say no by quickly giving your mind something else to do. Don't wait until your imagination, your body, and your hormones are involved. Pushing away at that point becomes that much harder.

Trying to outweigh a babbling, luscious, incoherent thought merely by thinking about your golf scores can result in that tiresome mental tug of war we all know and love: the rationalizations counteracted by the stern warnings, the fantasies limply protested by the good intentions, and back and forth. This frequently concludes with frustrated resignation into the arms of personal defeat and "just this once, okay?" And you hate yourself for it.

Out of Your Mind, Quick!

In order to distract the mind quickly and effectively from unneeded aggravation, you need to invoke a more powerful ally: your body.

When an unwanted thought intrudes, don't waste time and energy debating with it. Fill your mind's capacity with the distraction of a simple physical activity done with awareness. When a tempting thought intrudes use:

Inner Willpower Experience No. 9: The Body Block

Move from the fantasies of your mind into your present physical reality. Become aware of your surroundings, the room or place that you are in. Be there. Become aware of the present moment.

Become aware of your breathing. Breathe consciously.

Now do the very least action you need to do; do any form of physical activity, but with full attention and awareness. You might try any, or all, of the following:

Wiggle your toes slowly up and down. Feel the shoe leather. Feel your toe muscles flex.

Flex your ankles, rolling them from one side to the other and feeling the change in the position of your feet. Feel the stretch into your calves.

* * *

Make a fist. Open it and close it, pressing each finger against your palm one at a time, feeling the difference between each finger.

Look over the menu, or the buffet, for the most delicious thing you can eat that's within your guidelines. Look for something specific. Select it and enjoy it.

Reach for some mints. Unwrap them carefully. Notice the colors on the package. Feel the weight of the package in your hand.

Pick up a pen and write a letter.

Stand up, or sit down.

Smile, and walk away.

Excuse yourself and make a phone call.

The more completely you can involve your body in the action, the more effective it is for thought-stopping.

Whatever you do, do it with full awareness. Focus on the activity completely, fill your body and your mind with it. Repeat it as many times as necessary, then move on toward whatever else you need to do to get yourself away from whatever you want to avoid.

Sometimes, you might want to follow up with some pleasurable activity that will occupy at least a half hour of your time.

- Make a phone call to a good friend.
- Take a walk.
- Restyle your hair.

- Go to a movie.
- Read something lurid or funny.
- Sort out a drawer.
- Snuggle with your mate.

It doesn't matter what you do, as long as the activity will occupy your body and mind sufficiently to distract you completely from what should be a long-gone temptation, at least until the next time.

And the next time it happens, you'll have the extra inner strength and self-assurance of knowing that you've put the thing aside before. You'll be building confidence in your own inner willpower.

Binge-Proofing

What about binges—those out-of-control times that can leave your self-confidence and morale severely shaken? What can you do to help yourself when you seem bent on self-destruction? You can turn the binge into a learning experience by using your new tool, awareness, which will help you gain more control in the future.

Awareness is a powerful antidote to binging because the consciousness it brings to you is the exact opposite of what you seek when you binge. In a binge, we want only oblivion. We want to lose awareness of ourselves through too much food, drink, drugs, spending, or other excess. It isn't the food that we crave, it's the loss of other sensations, perhaps pain or anger or fear. In binging, we seek something—perhaps love or self-acceptance or stability—that the food or drink itself cannot really provide. So we settle for oblivion: choosing to feel nothing at all except possibly guilt, self-hatred, and remorse.

Here's some good binge therapy to use next time you need it.

Willpower Binging

The next time you begin to binge, simply remain aware: experience yourself, and whatever you are abusing, as fully as you can. Be total. Be there with as much totality and commitment as you can muster.

Do what you would normally do, but feel and experience everything, every moment, for as long as you can. Feel everything that is happening to you, and within you. Feel the changes. Remain conscious, remain totally aware. I want you to be 100 percent fully "with" whatever you are doing.

See if whatever you are actually experiencing is as good as the expectations and fantasies you had before you began. See how you feel when you finish.

Using Binge Awareness

If you can remain aware you will eventually bring the binging under your control. You will begin to see the activity for what it is, no more and no less, and become better able to choose your actions in the future.

You cannot really renounce something from your life until you have experienced it fully, until it has lost its value to you and you are ready to move on. The fastest way to let go of binging is to experience it totally.

Some people call this "hitting bottom," but that doesn't mean you have to reach some sordid external state before you can let go of something. It only means that you must reach the limits of the experience to understand that it holds no other answers for you. You must, as you have learned here, accept what your awareness has shown you.

But don't take my word for it: try it for yourself the next time you choose to step outside of your personal guidelines. The source of your awareness and self-acceptance—love—will always be waiting for you with its own safety net, if you let it.

After a conscious binge, you may notice that some of your attitudes toward whatever you chose as the vehicle for your attempted oblivion may begin to change. It may not happen all at once. But trust that it *is* happening for you, as long as you remain aware.

Sometimes feelings of disgust and self-hatred may emerge after a binge. Just acknowledge them, and let them go. They can't help you. Focus instead on all the minutes, hours, or days that you've done right for yourself. That time belongs to you, too.

When you're learning inner willpower, remember that it's not how many times you fall that matters; it's how many times you get up again. As long as you get up one more time than you fall, you're ahead of the game. Your inner willpower is gaining in strength.

11
Using Habit Power

Habits have a life of their own. Habit power will carry you when motivation or emotion or "sheer willpower" won't. Habits get things done easily, automatically, and in spite of the way you may be feeling that day. In fact, one of the key objectives of your inner willpower project is to raise your willpower activities to the status of habits.

The Helpful Trolls in Your Life

Habits aren't all negative. They can also be cheerful, eager, and incredibly hard-working little trolls that carry you—sometimes kicking and screaming—through your day. Habits open your eyes in the morning and move you toward the soap in the bathroom, the coffee in the kitchen, and the 7:46 train at the station. Have you ever noticed how, no matter what happens to change your routine in the morning, you always seem to get out the door at exactly the same time every day? That's habit power at work.

Habits probably park your car, push the correct elevator button and structure your let's-get-down-to-it office warm-up. They give you your reaction to the first problem of the day, remind you to eat lunch (they may even decide the menu), and cause you to punch the correct elevator button when you leave.

All along the way, habits have been invisibly supporting your personal concept of "the way I do what I do" to get those things done. Strong personal habits enable you to coast through a lot of the daily drudgery of actually getting done what you want to do. That's why habits are a powerful ally of your inner willpower.

One of the big reasons for suggesting that your inner willpower project provides a daily opportunity for action is to give you the advantages of building habit power right from the start. The purpose is to get those things you've chosen for yourself to the point where they've become a natural and reasonably effortless part of your life.

A daily schedule isn't a trap; it's breathing space for your personal growth. In the best of all possible worlds, those things that you think you need willpower for will simply become an ordinary, routine part of your life: something that you work with naturally, instead of fighting against.

THE CUES TO SUCCESS

Habits make powerful use of external environmental cues and associations. If you set up a pattern of activity in a certain specific environment, say, by going to the gym and starting your exercise program by walking briskly into the weight room and spending a concentrated half hour working on a routine that's appropriate for your level, or by always running around the reservoir at half speed when you get to the end of the park, you'll quickly set up subconscious cues and associations for yourself when you enter the gym or the park that put your body into a state that settles easily into the expected gymnasium workout or jog.

By the same token, if you come into the gym—the first few

times having dawdled in the locker room for a half hour—and you spend the first twenty minutes of your workout time examining the pores of your skin or the flab on your thighs in the mirror, then you shouldn't be surprised that it doesn't take long for your body to begin expecting that when you enter this environment, it's not really going to do anything but dither around for an hour or so and take a few halfhearted swats at the equipment.

This is equally true for habits of procrastination in familiar environments, like your home or office. You've set up a familiar series of cues when you return to your office from lunch, glance at your pile of phone messages, toss them back onto the desk with a grimace, and walk back out into the hall in search of the coffee pot or a friendly face. Your body *knows* it's supposed to avoid those phones messages for the next half hour or more, and that it can do almost anything except sit down and dial one of those numbers.

While you can immediately appreciate the "muscle memory" stimulus that those first few gym workouts gave to your later diligence in going through your weight training program, you can also see the unwitting help you've been giving your habit of procrastination by triggering all those usual associations in the office. No wonder the more you dither the worse it gets.

There's a good chance that many of your habits were never conscious decisions at all, but just simple repetitions of a convenient action. It doesn't matter. Your ever-eager brain and muscle memory accepted the input as solemnly as though it was your most carefully made choice, and built it into your circuitry with an efficiency and effectiveness that is one of Mother Nature's true miracles.

MAKING A FRESH START

One of the quickest ways to free yourself from past associations is to change your environment. Does this mean you have to find a new job or get a new office to make a new start? Not quite. While you may find it useful to change your health club affiliation or the route of your daily jog to start a new habit pattern, changing your home or career isn't usually feasible.

All you have to do is rearrange your perception of your environment. You can make changes in those surroundings in such a way as to make a real impression on your neurons. Beginnings are important. Good beginnings are indispensable. And the method for doing this is as old and time-tested as humanity itself: you make a little ceremony.

As human beings, when we want to begin any new venture or phase in our lives—graduate from school, get married, get a job, a promotion, buy a house, start a business, retire, whatever—we instinctively feel the need for some kind of "occasion" or ritual whether traditional, like a wedding or christening, or informal, like a signature and handshake or a drink with friends or the purchase of a new set of clothes.

We instinctively mark the passing of an old phase and the beginning of a new one with a special moment, a gesture with which we permit ourselves to think and act differently. We begin to assume the trappings of a new way of life. We change the cues. We do something differently. We give ourselves permission to grow.

This next experience is fun. It carries its own sense of accomplishment.

Inner Willpower Experience No. 10: A Fresh Start

You're going to go to your desk in your office, or your fridge, or your workspace, or your gym bag, or wherever you'll need to be when you work on your inner willpower project, and somehow reorganize or rearrange or recue that space.

If you don't associate your new project with any particular place, look around and choose any personal drawer or closet or room that feels "stale" and seems to hold old aspects of yourself within it. Trust your instincts. The spot you choose will work perfectly.

Take a good look at your desk or place. See how much past inertia it represents. Feel how it no longer really represents the new you that you are becoming, and how you have become somehow different or fresher than it is.

Decide that by cleaning it and rearranging it, you will dispose of the old energies and associations that are no longer relevant to your life. Everything that you toss into the wastebasket and every bit of dust that you wipe from the surface will contain the old energies of procrastination and inertia, and they will be tossed away, leaving only a fresh and supportive environment for your new life.

Begin tossing useless items out and putting others away. Every time that you toss out a piece of paper, pretend it is old procrastination: crumple it up, acknowledge that it has no further value for you, and let it go. Toss clothes into the laundry with the same enthusiasm. They're going to have all the staleness rinsed out of them.

Remove anything from the environment that could be a distraction for you: irrelevant foods, reading matter, even sentimental items that drag you down.

Every time you put something away in another location, imagine that it is now a new cue for action in its new location: give it a tap or a pat as you set it down, as though charging it with fresh energy.

This may feel like play and exercise for your imagination, but on an inner level your mind and neurons will take the message and emotions here in an integrated activity. It works; six million years of human evolution can't be wrong.

Clean out all the old dust and vibes. Be as extensive as you wish, mentally dissolving away the old, outdated "you" as you go, tossing away old mental and emotional debris.

You don't need to have any specific ideas about just what, exactly, is outdated about yourself. Your mind keeps very careful tabs on all your internal mental garbage and knows exactly how to drop what you no longer need. Just set it in motion with your external action. The inner "housecleaning" will happen automatically.

Once you've tossed all the old, set some fresh cues by rearranging what's still there. Move the things on your desk around to new locations, move the pictures on the wall or the placement of your chairs, if you can. Give yourself some new visual cues for your new habit patterns. Think about how you're setting your new inner willpower in place here.

Finally, bring in something new. New stationery, or pencils or datebook or a vase or personal token. Just something you can set down with a pat and say: Well, things are different here now, and so am I.

Look around the space where you've been working and appreciate how, as the space has changed, so has something inside of you. You're ready for a fresh start.

* * *

Enhancing Your Habit Power

Samantha found this exercise very useful for her literary endeavors. "I moved my whole workspace from the bedroom into the living room, and rearranged everything. It gave me an opportunity to start over.

"I also discovered that if I made a point of sitting down at the word processor and immediately retrieving the last thing I wrote—instead of sitting down and sipping my coffee while I thought about who to phone—I could get into it much more easily.

"I can see now that the procrastination was just a routine—a habit. With my new start-up routine, writing a few pages every day is becoming a painless new part of my life."

You can easily adapt Samantha's discovery to your own inner willpower project by using The Beginning Bonanza, below. Why is it a bonanza? Because anything you invest in it now in your newly recued space will pay you back a thousandfold in the months ahead.

You're going to make a good beginning, and start a powerful new habit.

Inner Willpower Experience No. 11: The Fourteen-Day Beginning Bonanza

Make your inner willpower project your number one priority for the next two weeks. Focus on good beginnings, and good patterns. Set in motion the best, most enthusiastic "doing" of your project that you can manage.

Just do it, no matter what kind of excuses seem to crop up, no matter how you feel about it. Act as if you were an absolute champion. Play along.

* * *

1. Take several long, deep breaths.
2. Bring yourself into the present moment.
3. Go through the motions of your project, pretending that you're absolutely terrific at carrying out what you want to do.
4. Savor the satisfaction of accomplishment each time. Tell yourself how wonderful you really are.

Good Habits Grow, Too

After Margaret began gradually changing her diet to substitute high-fiber foods for the high-cholesterol ones she had been eating, she'd spend about six weeks paying very close attention to integrating each "new" food into her menu on a regular basis and about two months nurturing the new habit before making any further changes. But she still felt that it probably was not making much difference anyway.

"I always felt I was climbing uphill with nothing much to look forward to. But you know what? My body really surprised me. Without my really noticing, my taste in foods was actually changing quite a bit.

"Last week I had my first real piece of rich food in about ten weeks: a slice of chocolate truffle cake. To my amazement, it was awful! I could taste all the fat and sugar. I stopped eating it after a few bites, feeling completely satisfied. I didn't want it anymore. I hadn't realized that these new menu habits were really taking hold. It's great! Now I can look at those slices of cake and think: it probably doesn't taste as good as it looks. . . ."

Fred, meanwhile, was beginning to experience some of the benefits of his regular visits to the pool.

"Now I'm really beginning to notice if I don't work out. I feel cranky and out of sorts, like something's missing. The good feelings I have after swimming a few laps are starting to feel like the real me. This is quite an improvement."

12
Reorganizing Your Priorities

Clifford can remember the day he finally quit smoking like it was yesterday.

"All of a sudden, it was like I didn't need any willpower to do it. I just woke up one morning somehow convinced that I didn't want to smoke. I didn't need the cigarettes anymore. Bang. That was it. The rest—actually quitting—was easy."

Did Clifford feel motivated to quit? "It sure felt like it, but I'm not sure I can tell you where the motivation came from. I just knew I didn't want to smoke anymore."

When Clifford awoke that morning, he was aware that something had changed. But what? And how can you apply it to your own life?

Your Priorities Can Change

It's actually very simple: his priorities were new. Clifford had somehow rearranged his internal list of what was really important to him in his life. His inner nature was telling him that some of his old wants and needs had become less important to him now, and that new desires were waiting to be recognized and acted upon.

Once he had become aware of the new priorities of the present-day Clifford instead of the old Clifford, smoking no longer answered any important needs of the person he is today. His motivation was automatically redirected toward new goals.

Clifford didn't "stop smoking." Instead, he started "not smoking" and the cigarettes got left behind in the shuffle. He never had to fight with his habit. His energies simply went elsewhere, toward new things. Reorganizing your priorities is a powerful inner willpower tool.

Did you ever have a favorite toy when you were a child? There's probably a much-loved teddy or doll or bicycle somewhere in your youth. And when you were small, if someone had tried to take away your favorite thing, there probably would have been great distress and pain on your part, and a lasting sense of loss.

But do you remember the day you played with that beloved toy for the last time? Do you remember the day you put it aside forever? Not really, I'll bet. Probably not at all.

What happened that day? You'd discovered something better to do, that's all. School, or cars, or teenage romance. You were hurrying toward something new in your life; you were becoming a different person. The toy was never really relinquished, only dropped somewhere lower and lower on your inner list of what mattered to you.

You're still growing and changing today. Your priorities are continually being reevaluated by your inner self. The difference now is that we don't always acknowledge these inner changes very quickly. We let them accumulate until we are no longer sure what we really want or who we are at all. We lose touch with our true selves. And then we wake up one morning saying, "I need a new life. Or a new job. Maybe a new city. A new marriage? A new personality? I don't know *what* I want anymore." And midlife crisis chalks up another victim.

It doesn't have to be that way. By continually listening to the voice of your heart, to your inner beacon of truth and personal harmony, you can learn to refine and clarify your evolving sense of purpose. You can make far less disruptive ongoing changes in your external behavior that are in keeping with your true priorities and goals. You can learn to use your priorities to provide yourself with a steady supply of motivation and energy for your inner willpower.

Priorities Come from the Heart

It can be very easy to shape your external behavior when it is in keeping with your true inner needs. You are able to work most actively with yourself to become the person you really want to be when your head and your heart are in agreement as to what it is that you want in life.

That agreement must start from your heart, not your head. You must pursue the love of your heart with the diligence and common sense of your head, not the other way around.

There is no point in trying to understand our personal priorities by beginning with what you intellectually think you "should" want, or what you "ought to be" or "what others expect of me" or what "might be a good idea." Begin from inside your own heart. Trying to discover your inner priorities by looking outside of yourself to others is like losing a valuable coin on one side of the street but searching for it on the other because the light is better there.

Your relationship to your inner priorities, to your inner life, is probably the most intimate and personal relationship you can have. No other person, no outside source, can ever decide for you what is really important to you.

It's like falling in love. No matter how well-meaning your

friends or family may be about arranging dates or introductions for you to the "perfect person for you," only you can decide if and when you will fall in love with someone. No matter how well anyone may understand you or how much they may love you, only you can know the true answer of your own heart. And that is your absolute right and privilege as a human being.

Your heart is your own sanctuary. You are the only person who has the key. And it is from the heart that you must begin to decide what it is that you truly want.

Coming from Your Own Heart

Coming from your heart means living in the moment, feeling the experience first, and analyzing later. It means giving your mind some true and—yes—heartfelt data to work with. It means experience first, and ask questions and evaluate later.

The heart doesn't always speak to you in words, as the mind does. The heart speaks with a kind of inner knowing, a voice of pure certainty that only you can understand, and respond to. Your mind can sometimes tell you lies and half-truths created from incomplete data, hopes and fears, and the world outside of you, but the heart knows only itself. It is your inner link to a much wider world of truth and personal serenity. And it is from the heart that your personal priorities can speak most clearly.

The next two Inner Willpower Experiences are a simple, direct way to review and, if you'd like, reorganize or reevaluate your personal priorities. I suggest that you do these together, in sequence. The ideas that they generate will begin to percolate through your consciousness over the next few days or weeks, and they will give you some fresh insights into what's currently important to you.

You may want to sit down in the very near future and do these experiences again. Many things that may seem foggy to you right now will have become much clearer and more meaningful by then. It's a natural process, set in motion by your having chosen to focus your attention on this area of your inner self.

We'll begin with the refreshing Body of Light Experience, and continue right along with the valuable Three Wishes Experience.

Inner Willpower Experience No. 12: Body of Light

You may recall how you created your comfortable place, by looking around you and focusing on the stillness of your surroundings, then by focusing on your breathing. Use any of the Present Moment techniques. Refresh your memory by turning back to page 9 and following along until you feel relaxed and comfortable. Don't rush ahead; you can't get the real benefit of these exercises until you are in a relaxed, balanced state of Present Moment awareness.

Still breathing in a relaxed manner, allow the focus of your attention to shift to your belly, to your hara center. Simply become aware of your midsection, enter inside of it, notice what it feels like. Full? Empty? Gurgling? Tight? Loose? Light? Heavy? Warm? Cool? What? Just notice, that's all.

Allow the breath to rise and fall naturally through the hara center. Let go; let your belly expand and relax as it needs to. Take as much time as you need to "visit" your hara center; it could probably use some tender-loving attention from you.

Begin to breathe a bit more deeply, in a relaxed fashion. Allow each outward breath to release the tension, the mixed feelings in your hara center. Feel that each outward breath is expelling all the cloudiness, the darkness, the staleness inside of you. Imagine everything old flowing away from you: out of your center, out of your bones, out of your cells, out of your pores. Let it all go. Breathe it out and away. Let the staleness vanish like darkness when you have turned on a light. Let it wash away from you completely. Take as much time as you need.

Now begin to fill your body with light. Imagine that each incoming breath brings in sparkling freshness, brings new energy in the form of glowing, golden light.

See the light as soft and pleasant like the light of the morning sun. Feel how each cell and each pore and each bone begins to respond to this light. Feel how eagerly they begin to open and relax into the light of your incoming breath.

Feel how the light is filling your chest, and gently nourishing your heart. Allow your heart to bathe in protective, strengthening light. Feel how it opens in response. Take your time.

Allow all your cells to bask in this crystalline light. It feels good. It feels safe and secure. Each cell is filled with beautiful, clear light.

Allow the crystalline radiance to fill you completely, so that your body becomes clearer and brighter with each incoming breath. Breathe.

Allow your body to *become* the light. Let its radiance and clarity increase with each breath, until in your mind's eye you seem to be made of crystalline glow, of pure inner clarity. Take your time.

Allow your brain and your emotions to share this clarity. Let them bathe in the glow of clear, true light, and come to rest within it. Feel how the energy of your center is actually becoming clearer and more peaceful.

* * *

In this clarity, your inner heart understands your life, now. Feel how the energy of your heart has grown clear and true and serene. Feel that your heart's knowledge can speak directly, clearly, and simply now.

Sit quietly. Be at rest. Know that you are truly in touch with your inner core and able to listen to your heart's eloquent, wordless message. Be at peace with yourself.

When you are ready, gently begin the following Three Wishes Experience. Begin to listen to your heart's true desires.

The second experience is a paper and pencil exercise. Here, a few sheets of paper can become an enormously valuable inner willpower tool. Don't be afraid to scribble, cross things out, or misspell words; no one is going to grade you on this. It's just for you.

Jotting down notes as you think is a tremendously powerful way to discover just what you *really* think about something, since meanings very often don't come clear until they are literally staring you in the face. Paper's cheap; you can rip it up later, or save it for a rainy day. But the lessons are irreplaceable. So take a few minutes, grab a paper and pencil, and curl up in your comfortable corner.

Inner Willpower Experience No. 13: Three Wishes

Suppose you could have three wishes for yourself—not for the world at large, but for your life, for you. What do you really want, if you could do or be or have anything right now? Never mind how likely: What turns you on? What do you care about? What do you daydream about most often? What do you love and respond to?

* * *

You might begin by making a list that says: Happiness is . . . to start you thinking. Jot down a list of those things that make you happy or give you personal satisfaction. Or, suppose you could look at your life from its conclusion: What would you most want to have done? What would have really mattered to you? Spend some time choosing three wonderful wishes.

Put down this book and spend a few minutes writing. Go ahead. Just get started. Write something, anything. This is important.

Now that you're thinking, are there more than three wishes? Good! Jot them down. Keep writing, as many as you'd like. Take your time. Make a generous list.

Look at your whole list and notice which wishes really excite you. Flesh them out. Use more paper.

Next, out of this whole list, choose your three—or so—favorite wishes.

What is this list telling you about your priorities? Do any of your favorite wishes qualify as something you've thought you wanted willpower for? Where do those willpower projects really rank in your life? In other words, how badly do you really want to do some of the things you've been telling yourself you want to do? Are these your priorities, or someone else's?

What do you want to do instead? Take your time, think about it. This is heavy-duty willpower fuel you're making here. Browse back over your list; make a fresh list of priorities, if you'd like.

When you're ready, take a look at how you spent your day today, and this past week. How are your most important goals and priorities being expressed in your life right now, in terms of how you actually allocate your time, or how you actually behave? What changes would you like to make?

Where can you find the time to act according to your priorities? You may feel your life is not your own and that you have many, many obligations impinging on your time. But let's put aside the question of career or job changes at this time, and assume you'll have to spend most of your day working somehow. Now what? Family and household obligations. Let's assume you don't want to make any changes here.

That probably leaves you with a couple of hours of watching television time. Is every program you watch on TV more important to you in terms of your priorities than some of the other goals you've listed? What do you really want to do in your life right now?

This is the central question: What do you really *want* from life? What are your true priorities? Can you put them into words? Try, just for yourself.

Maybe at this point it's just feelings, longings, or tears. That's okay. It's powerful to feel these things. What you're really experiencing is the full force of your inner willpower.

Let these feelings carry you along for the next few minutes if they arise. Let them flow out; they won't last long. It's important to allow yourself to really want what you want for your life. To feel how powerfully these desires hold you, to really know how much it matters to you.

Know this to be true: whatever you want for your life *does* matter. It *is* important, no matter what your goals are. You have as much right to your goals and priorities as any other creature on earth.

These needs are intimately tied to your reasons for being born, to the reasons for your entire life. They matter.

And don't be fooled into thinking that you "should" have "better" or "higher" priorities than those you feel most strongly in your life right now. That's not the point. Begin from where you are, remember? Do what is relevant in your life right now, and know that as you reach these goals higher ones will come into view. They're only signposts on your path after all, aren't they? Trust yourself and your needs. It's okay to want what you want.

Maybe you'd like to take a walk and think about this list? It's important; take your time. You've covered some very important ground here.

13
Motivation Is Personal Fuel

Motivation—the energy of desire—arises out of your personal priorities.

Motivation is really a kind of translation of those priorities into something that is useful to you right now: that immediate reward or boost of energy that comes from connecting your actions to something that is satisfying or meaningful to you right on the spot.

When you become more aware of the different things that might motivate you, in different ways at different times, you can consciously use your motives to help keep your actions in line with your true priorities.

Motives are an intensely personal fuel. They must matter to you, not to anyone else. They must be ideas or feelings that come from an inner priority that's important to you right now. And you're the only person who can decide what that priority really is. Motives simply "click" with your inner being, your higher self. They feel good. They have energy for you.

No other person, no matter how close they may be to you, or how eloquent and persuasive a speaker, can really "motivate" you unless what they're saying has some resonance to your inner priorities. In effect, that outside speaker merely reminds you of a motivation that was already there inside of you, waiting to be called upon.

Motives of all kinds can be useful at various times in moving the same task forward. Different motivators may work at different times for you on the same inner willpower project.

If you think of motives as a secret arsenal for getting you moving when you need it, becoming aware of some useful motives is rather like reviewing your collection of tools and deciding which one you'll use today. It's nice to know what your options are. Especially when you "don't feel motivated." Or when the catalog photo of a skinny woman in a bathing suit you've taped to your fridge doesn't do it any more.

Rationalizations Weaken You

Having an arsenal of personal motives will also keep you from complicating your life with rationalizations and justifications for staying trapped in bad habits.

Rationalization means attributing your actions to reasons that have nothing to do with your real motives. How do you tell a rationalization from a motivation? It's easy to let your body tell you. You can check in with your hara. See whether whatever you're telling yourself feels good and true, or feels somehow uncomfortable and false.

Rationalizations also reveal themselves by showing up *after* you've decided to do something instead of before: you don't want to go to the gym, so you tell yourself it's too late to go anyway, or you feel a cold coming on and you'd better take care of it . . . or. . . . A rationalization always tries to build a bridge back to hara comfort and balance after you've chosen to do something that your body knows is out of line with your true well-being and priorities.

A motive, no matter what it may be, is always something that your body can recognize as truth and accept as fuel for action.

Motives Come in Every Shape and Color

One of the important things to understand about motives is that there is rarely a single, clear-cut motive driving you. You can have several motives operating simultaneously at a number of different levels from, for instance, a fairly primitive kind of revenge ("They'll be green with envy.") to seeking lofty brownie points ("The very saints in heaven will be so pleased.") to the truly noble ("Because it's the right thing to do, even if no one else knows.")

Motives can be very simple ("Because I like it and I want it." or "I'm going to be gorgeous."). They can be rather convoluted ("I never really said this to my father when he was alive, but somehow I've always felt that . . .") They can inspire ("I'm going to be successful like her someday.") or goad (". . . or you'll turn into a fat slob and people will laugh at you."). Motives can be externally driven ("They're watching me.") or internal ("It's good for me." or "I'm going to have so much fun!")

Motives can cover the whole range of Deadly Sins: pride, greed, envy, lust, sloth, anger, and gluttony. They can also encompass the Virtues, most notably love, compassion, justice, truth, and honor.

Motives can be blended, and sometimes honor exists side by side with pride (as in "What will people think of me?"), but it's powerful just the same.

Long Haul Versus Short-Term Motives

What you may have noticed, though, about lesser motives like anger, embarrassment, or vanity, is that while they may have a great deal of immediate impulse power, they don't necessarily sustain you for the long haul. They get tired pretty fast.

Anger, especially, tends to burn itself out pretty quickly. It won't really carry you the distance. And continually trying to rouse yourself to a pitch of foaming anger in order to get something done will only burn you out.

That's where the higher, or greater, motives come into their own. Great motives, such as love of humanity or your family or the planet, or respect for one's body as the supreme expression of Mother Nature's gifts, or striving for excellence for its own sake, don't necessarily have the emotional glamour of good old-fashioned greed. But they do provide long-term staying power for willpower tasks that may require a lifetime to master.

And they are mighty comforting in those three A.M.'s of the soul, when "Why the hell am I doing this?" doesn't seem to have a ready answer. They feel good inside. They remind you of your better traits. They let you stand a little taller, and live another day.

What Does Enthusiasm Have to Do With It?

Enthusiasm is, unfortunately, rarely a motive for getting something done. Enthusiasm is a wonderful emotion, a terrific feeling and a great source of energy. The power of emotional impulse—that "do it now!" burst—can really get you moving. It's great. But like all emotions, enthusiasm tends to come and go of its own accord. And it has a perverse way of not being around when you really need it.

Expecting to feel enthusiastic is actually something of a trap. When you undertake any program of self-improvement, even one that's in line with all your goals and priorities—you don't have to feel enthusiastic about it all the time. There will be days—Lord knows—when you absolutely loathe going to the gym or eating your veggies.

Does Guilt Motivate?

Guilt does not play much of a role as a useful motive either. It is only useful if you can draw on a simple moment of regret to inspire real change in your actions, and let that moment of insight become the end of the guilt, right there. If you can drop the guilt and go on with your life you are an exceptionally practical, mentally healthy person.

Most of us can decide to use guilt as a weapon against ourselves. We believe that the more guilt we can feel, the better we must "really" be. We think that since the "real me" disapproves of our actions, the person who did them wasn't us anyway and we can therefore reject that "other" person easily. So we give that "other" person a good, hard shove.

But that "other" person is you, too. You, feeling the pain of rejection. You, denied the energy and support of your own love. You, mired in an endless swamp of pointless recrimination and nonacceptance. You, stripped of self-esteem and confidence. What are you accomplishing by feeling guilty?

Keeping in mind an image of what you'd like to become can be very inspiring and you should use it that way. But don't make the mistake of tossing out the real person sitting there in your chair right now when you do. Guilt is basically useless. Let your motives come from love, not self-hatred.

Take yourself gently in hand, and accept your own behavior as part of who you actually are right now. Be where you are. Then you can begin making constructive changes and get on with your life.

Using Motives as a tool

Unlocking your arsenal of motives means, most of all, being candid with yourself. There's something in each of us that responds to the idea that "I never do anything except for the highest and purest and noblest motives. . . ." That's a very valuable inner reminder that there are, indeed, noble motives within you to aspire to, and to inspire you. But sometimes it can be very practical to use your "unworthy" motives as well, like greed or revenge or envy, if they will get you moving in the right direction. You're entitled to have both.

The important thing is that you use motives consciously, with full awareness that you're using a tool to get a job done, and acknowledging that using a tacky motive does not make you a rotten person, it only gets you to walk past the pastry counter and out the door. Becoming conscious and aware of your actions and feelings in the present moment is the critical willpower skill. Learning to recognize and use your motives is another "angle" on learning to use the present moment.

FINDING USEFUL MOTIVES

This next experience will produce an inventory of handy motives you can save for a rainy day.

Inner Willpower Experience No. 14: Just Because

From your previous list of priorities, choose one or two that you'd like to work on. You can follow up on the others whenever you'd like.

At the top of a fresh sheet of paper write: I'd like to (your priority) because . . . Writing this down will help keep you focused on this priority while you follow this experience.

Now simply begin to list the advantages or benefits that will come to you from pursuing this priority, whatever those benefits may be. They may be big or small, physical or emotional, tangible or ephemeral, silly or personal, long-term or immediate. Jot down all the things that might, at various times, motivate you to act.

List good reasons, personal reasons, silly reasons, obvious reasons, obscure and petty reasons. You may invent reasons that no one might ever really want to use, but jot them down anyway.

* * *

To start you off, ask yourself things like: What are the advantages for: me? him? her? them? the future? my looks? my body? my health? What about personal comfort? pain? money? status? sensuality? "goodness"? "badness"? revenge? dislike? ridicule? fear? punishment? fun? excitement? security? power? control? challenge? creativity? esthetic reasons? joy? future benefit? higher reward? love? inner peace? make someone happy? make myself happy? they deserve it? I deserve it? Just because I want it? What else?

If saying to yourself "I want to do this because . . ." doesn't tell you enough, ask yourself: Why would someone else want to do this? What would be the advantages to someone else in my position?

Keep writing; this is quantity, not quality. List *all* the advantages.

You may notice that some of these advantages get a real "Aha!" from you when you write them down. Some may seem kind of speculative, but some others feel really good right away. Some might make you laugh out loud. Some might make you cringe, feeling a bit queasy in your hara. That's good, in its own way, because it alerts you to the fact that this motive holds some emotional energy for you.

Keep writing. As you get to the bottom of the page, or the next page, you may notice that the character of your reasons and advantages has changed somewhat, and perhaps you're writing with a bit more feeling or caring. Perhaps some of the things you jotted down earlier get written again, but with new meaning. Or the reasons no longer seem to have anything to "do" with your original priority. That's okay.

Is a new layer of motivation emerging? What else do you care about? Keep writing until you've said it all.

* * *

Now put a check mark beside all the reasons on your list that stand out for you, either because they feel good or feel uncomfortable.

Review your list, feeling whatever emotions some of these ideas may generate. Is there anything else to add? Anything that you wanted to say but didn't? Put it down, even if it doesn't seem very important.

Now, what have you learned here? What are your lists telling you that might come in handy in the future? Take your time, read through them again. There may be some new ideas cropping up here. Or a single word that tugs at your heart in a new way. Just let any emotions or feelings you may have right now flow naturally.

When you're ready, this might be a really good time to get up and go for another walk, or go look out the window for awhile. You've covered a lot of ground here. You've started to feel some of the power of your own personal desire for something in your life. Feel it deeply; savor it. These feelings and motives, and your ability to call on them later, will carry you a long, long way toward your dream.

Go ahead: spend some time reviewing your lists. It's good for you. Go to bed early, if you can, and sleep well tonight. You've earned it. Things will seem much clearer in the morning.

14
Affirming Your Inner Strengths

Right now, in your life, there's a tiny seedling of a new, better you that's sprouting and is beginning to unfurl into the light. Whether or not you realize it, you are becoming a better person. It is really happening.

This tiny seedling of inner development has all the potential to grow into a wonderful, strong, flourishing and happy person: your own best self, the you that you'd like to be. But like any new planting, this one requires tender protection from rough-shod treatment, plenty of thoughtful sunshine, nourishment, and safe space to grow in. You've got to pay extra attention to tending your new inner self in these early days, and be sure that you "feed" your new life the best food to grow on.

Affirming Your Strengths

That's what the fourth inner willpower skill—positive affirmation—is all about. Positive, constructive affirmations act like plant food for a better life. They are a special rich mix designed for strong, flourishing growth. They reinforce your better activities, encourage you, and increase your self-esteem and self-confidence. The more positive affirmations you choose to feed yourself, the better you'll grow.

Positive affirmation is the deliberate emphasis on positive thoughts and emotional attitudes. Affirmations are those thoughts and feelings you use to confirm to yourself that "that's what life is like, that's the way it is, and that's the truth." They act as your brain's feedback or confirmation of reality. They form a major part of your constant interior monologue—what you say to yourself automatically—and of your feelings or reactions to your experiences. Affirmations can take the form of words and phrases, or they can be simply fleeting feelings—an internal shrug or smile. They can be positive or negative.

Here are some examples of positive affirmations:

> I feel great.
> I'm as healthy as can be.
> I'm taking better care of myself.
> I only eat what's good for me.
> I'm always on time.
> I exercise every day.
> I have more and more energy all the time.
> Cigarettes bore me.
> I feel great when I'm sober.
> I'm relaxed and in control of myself.

Are any of these affirmations "true" for you right now? It doesn't matter. They'll work anyway. Whenever you affirm a positive message to yourself it really doesn't matter if most of your present behavior is not what you want it to be. It doesn't matter if your present behavior bears no resemblance at all to what you want *because affirmation doesn't work with what is, but what will be.* Affirmation shapes future growth. Affirmation is what allows you to become what you want to be.

Affirmations work. You've probably been unwittingly using affirmations all your life, and over the years they've played a powerful role in shaping your present self. But, like most people, you've probably been using negative affirmations to confirm your weaknesses rather than to build your strengths. You've been powerfully reinforcing the negatives, unwittingly increasing their dominance in your life by telling yourself negative affirmations like:

I'm so clumsy.
No matter how much I diet, the weight comes right back.
I get so depressed.
I'm not very good with numbers.
I can't get organized.
I can't work until I've had my coffee.
I need a drink.
I'd like to stop smoking, but I can't seem to quit.
Nothing ever works out.
Here goes nothing.
That's just my luck.

YOUR BRAIN IS LISTENING

Affirmations are literal commands to your brain. Your brain—and your body eventually—respond quite literally to whatever it believes to be true. And that's whatever you *tell* yourself is true. Whenever you repeat to yourself: "I can never remember people's names!" your brain just says: "Right. Okay. I can never remember names. Forget this name I've just been introduced to. Blank. Done, yes sir. I can never remember names."

If you'd been telling yourself "It'll come to me!" eventually the name would. Your brain's been instructed to retrieve the person's name.

If you begin to listen to yourself, you may be amazed at how many literal commands you give yourself throughout the day to fail, forget, screw up, or become angry, frustrated, and miserable.

A neighbor of mine even literally made himself ill with negative affirmations. Arthur is a brilliant telecommunications designer who is inexplicably going deaf. No question, it is not imaginary. The sensitive bones in his ear are hardening and fusing, but the doctors can not find a cure.

One day, while we sat around the pool, another neighbor began to propose some changes in a plan of Arthur's. Arthur abruptly cut him off. And do you know what he said? "I don't want to hear that." With a shock, I remembered: he says that all the time! I don't want to hear that. His body, after years and years of this input, was doing exactly what it had been told. It was a dramatic example of affirmation at work. But sadly, Arthur "didn't want to hear" about affirmations, either. As far as I know, his hearing is still declining.

Your Willing Brain

Your brain is both smarter and dumber than it appears to be. Smarter, because it can process a tremendous amount of incoming information at multiple levels that you're never consciously aware of, and give you the benefit of that knowledge. But dumber, because your brain has no idea whether incoming information is true or not. That's a fact. Your brain can only decide whether incoming data matches previous data and experience. That makes it "true" or "false" as far as your brain is concerned. But that also means that your brain is tremendously contextual, subjective, and easily biased. It only "knows" what's already in it.

So when you affirm—or tell yourself—something, it doesn't matter whether it's externally true or not right now. It only matters that your brain believes it. And your brain *will* begin to believe whatever it hears often enough. Eventually the new positive data that you've chosen to feed yourself will outweigh the old data and become your new standard for deciding "truth." Your brain will go to work to bring your body—and your life—into line with your new beliefs. You'll be using your brain as a powerful ally of your good intentions, instead of as an unintended roadblock.

While we may hesitate to tell ourselves positive things, we are usually all too willing to believe the bad things. Negative affirmations can unintentionally weave themselves through our whole thought process. They can become whole programs, long tapes that our brains will replay throughout the day.

These programs are usually stern lectures or convenient rationalizations. We automatically use them to punish ourselves. But like the guilt they are meant to evoke, these negative affirmations only succeed in tying us ever more strongly to negative behavior. This is mainly because negative affirmations succeed in persuading you that you are not—or could not be—any better or different than you are right now. Negative affirmations set up artificial prison bars and then forget to tell you that you have the key in your pocket! You never bother to try opening the prison door because you assume that you can't, or shouldn't. What you don't consciously realize is that you've built the prison yourself.

Your Brain's Greatest Hits

Perhaps you'll recognize some of these popular negative affirmation programs. We'll talk later about how to dump them from your life, but let's first become aware of:

The Bitch

You slob! Can't you ever do anything right? You're such a jerk, you're always late, you're always forgetting things, you look like a mess, you loser. You think you're such hot stuff? Look at you: eating like a pig. You're lazy, you never finish what you start . . . .

The Bitch inside of you can do a far more devastating job on your self-image than even your severest external critic, because the voice in your head never quits, never misses an opportunity to undermine you, and always goes for the kill. The Bitch tells you that you are nothing. And you believe it, and act on it.

The important thing to understand about The Bitch is that you have created it. It isn't anybody real—even if you may have a few people in mind that it resembles. It's a program that you have built through use and repetition. It's a synthetic creation of your own mind that you have accepted as real.

The Whino

Ooooh, I don't feel so good today ... I think I have a cold coming on ... My back's acting up ... I can't handle stress ... What do you expect at my age? I don't have the energy I used to ... I don't sleep so well ... I keep forgetting ... I tire so easily ... What's the use? Poor me ...

The Whino keeps you in prison by continually repeating and reinforcing negative commands to your body. These weaknesses can then serve as a convenient rationalization or excuse for not making any changes, or for skipping your walk or bike ride, or for having that extra helping or "just one."

The Whino is a particularly insidious creation because it lets you believe you can't feel happy unless you are somehow miserable. It gives you permission to be nice to yourself—there's nothing wrong with that—but only by taking away your freedom to act constructively. It tells you that the only good things you can do for yourself are contained in times of weakness, illness, insecurity, and unhappiness. You can't feel good unless you're feeling bad.

* * *

The Plumed Serpent

Mmmmm ... This is so comfortable right here on this couch.... Why don't we just have another? Who needs that silly fresh air anyway? You can do it later.... Mmmmm ... Sleep ... Sleep ...

The Plumed Serpent is the goddess of inertia, the guardian of procrastination, wrapped in the potent bait of the sensuality of the present moment. There's nothing wrong with sensuality, far from it. But The Plumed Serpent imprisons you by convincing you that the *only* sensuality lies in what you're doing right now, which is usually nothing.

Fact is, the sensuality of the present moment is always available to you in every activity, once you become aware of it. And by sensuality I don't mean just sexuality. I mean all forms of pleasant sensation and experience. Sexuality is certainly sensual, but you're missing out on a lot of pleasure in life if you limit your definition.

When you listen to The Plumed Serpent, you give up the opportunities for the deeper sensuality that come with better health, more personal accomplishment, and greater self-confidence. As you become a stronger and happier person, your ability to experience life will become greater, not less. Don't let The Plumed Serpent cheat you.

Ultimate Doom

God's gonna punish you for this. You have no right to happiness. You'll pay for being happy. Your mother's watching. Don't you know how many unhappy people there are in the world? How dare you feel good! Better screw up right now.

This one's spooky: retribution raised to karmic and cosmic levels—the Ultimate Authority saying that you are so horrible you don't deserve anything but misery. What makes it especially insidious is that your mind has created Ultimate Doom—it isn't really the voice of the Creator—out of an incomplete understanding of the great universal laws of cause and effect.

Yes, good is rewarded and evil is punished. But whatever made you decide that you were evil? You've probably felt like that because your body and your emotions work in an interesting way here. You tend to retain the memory and imprint of negative, painful, evil experiences far more strongly and easily than you do of loving, happy, positive, good moments. Bad things make an impression in a way that good things don't.

Just for a moment, think back to some unpleasant experience or moment you've had recently: put yourself there, in that sad or angry or fearful place. See it, feel it, and be in it. Feel what this memory does to your hara right now, with just a little encouragement. It's a very strong sensation, isn't it?

Now, let go of that moment: just let it go. Breathe it out. Come back here.

Next, recall some pleasant or happy moment. Be in that place, and summon up the associated good feelings. Take your time. Experience it.

Much more subtle, no? Takes longer? More fleeting? Do you have to ask yourself: When was the last time I felt good? What *did* it feel like?

What Your Body Can't Hold

Negative emotions—anger, fear, jealously, hatred—are always stronger and easier to evoke than positive sensations like love, compassion, and bliss. That's just the way it is. Your body doesn't hold on to good feelings in the same way as it holds onto bad feelings.

That doesn't mean happiness doesn't exist, only that we don't focus on it in our emotional memories. Instead, we end up remembering an accumulated collection of Bad Moments, holding on to all the mistakes that anyone is bound to collect over one—or several—lifetimes. We can come to believe that we are only the bad things, and not the good because we can't get in touch with the good deeds as easily. We have an incomplete and erroneous view of what we really are.

If you mistakenly see yourself as being only the sum total of all those bad things, you can easily end up looking at yourself and thinking: Uh-oh.

But the Ultimate Doom program is not—repeat, *not*—the actual verdict on your life. Please allow yourself the space to believe that you simply don't know or don't remember all the good things about yourself. And that quite possibly you have a lot of good things coming your way that you deserve and have earned and can enjoy. Leave your mind open in this regard. It's okay. You really are free to create your own experience in the present moment.

Inner Willpower Experience No. 15: Thought Catching

For the next few days, simply begin to listen to yourself. Observe your reaction to life around you.

Become aware of your thoughts, your interior monologues. What do you tell yourself about life? About other people? About yourself?

What do you say to yourself when something good happens? When something bad happens? How do you react?

What do you say at the start of your day? What do you expect? What about before you fall asleep at night?

Just observe, just let your thoughts and reactions flow naturally. Become aware, that's all. Listen to yourself.

* * *

After a few days, ask: What are you feeding yourself? Are your thoughts about yourself and your life mostly positive? Or mostly negative?

If you're like most people, you'll gradually become aware of the huge diet of negative, pessimistic thoughts that are constantly on tap in your messages to yourself. You might become aware of some of it right away. Other more subtle negative messages—they're really more like negative expectations—can provide a wash of color over your thoughts that doesn't really become evident until you've begun to improve your outlook with some positive affirmations.

You don't need to root out every single negative attitude now. Simply become aware that some of the obstacles you've been facing may in fact be creations of your own affirmations. And that you have the ability to choose what you will affirm: either the positive or the negative.

15
Affirmations: Not Just Words, but Music

What makes a good positive affirmation?

The choice of good words or images to create a good positive affirmation is reasonably important. However, it doesn't really matter because the subjective *feeling* behind the words is what is of paramount importance.

Let's start with the good words. Remember, as we learned earlier, that the brain is not very good with "try not to" commands, and that such instructions can frequently lead the brain right into the path of the metaphorical elephant rather than away from it. This means that affirmations such as:

I don't smoke.
I never overeat.
I don't procrastinate.

are actually less effective than the positively phrased:

I feel wonderful without cigarettes.
I am completely satisfied when I eat moderately.
I'm always on schedule.

Positive affirmations always seek to express the good result as a tangible, real thing. They put a positive shape onto your desired results, rather than leave you with a mental void after you've banned the negative behavior. After all, if you think, for instance, about "not smoking" you may be summoning up an image of a frustrated, anxious chain-smoker nervously waiting out empty periods between smokes. Not very appealing, is it? On the other hand, saying "I'm a fresh air person" might create for you an image of someone healthy, energetic, and happy who naturally never smokes.

Of course, you don't need to tie yourself into a verbal pretzel avoiding negatives if the simple "I don't smoke" seems to have meaning and be effective for you. Use what's practical for you.

AFFIRMATIONS ARE RIGHT NOW

Second, good positive affirmation is always phrased in the present, not in the future. Instead of:

> Things will get easier.
> I'm going to start saving some money.
> Someday I'll be slender and healthy.

treat each idea as though it were *already* a fact, as though you could be the way you want to be right now, in the present. Rephrase these affirmations as:

> Things are getting easier.
> I always save 10 percent of my paycheck.
> I'm slender and healthy.

Never mind that you're overweight and miserable right now. Remember, we aren't talking about external reality here, but about the way that the brain programs itself.

The brain works in the present tense. The future is the brain's great never-never, and anything that you say about the future as "I will" or "someday" gets stored in never-never land. Say "I am" and the brain pays attention. The brain says, "I am? Yes sir. Hmmm, as I look around I don't see any of that right now, but I'll get right on it. Yes sir, I am."

And your brain will go to work to execute the program you've just given it with your affirmation. *It may take time,* and much repetition, before you see external results, but soon you'll begin to reap the benefits of your good affirmations just as surely as you've seen the results over time of the negative ones.

What You Feel Is What You Get

Third, the fastest route to your brain is through your feelings. If you say to yourself: "You're a success," but in a tone of voice that implies: "You miserable worthless scum," is the stronger message in the words or the feelings? The brain remembers what you feel about something far more strongly and easily than it remembers exact words.

Feelings release powerful neurohormones that provide the biochemical link to a thought or memory in the brain. Your brain can actually become addicted to positive or negative experiences because it relies on these neurohormones for stimulation. Which is why, even when you don't especially like some recurring negative experience in your life, you may come to feel that you actually need—or deserve—it. Your brain gets used to the stimulation.

The power of your feelings means that effective affirmations begin by being comfortable and positive about the good results you'd like to obtain. This means hooking your brain into the good results with a nice dose of pleasure neurohormones.

The easiest way to do this is by allowing yourself to experience the pleasurable feelings of your accomplishment *in the present* as you affirm it, just as though it was actually happening right now.

Yes: enjoy now, work later. It's much easier and more effective than saying, "Someday, when I'm finished, I'll feel great." Feel what you're affirming right now.

AFFIRMING YOUR INNER WILLPOWER

Start using positive affirmations in your life by giving yourself a very deliberate diet of them for a few weeks or months, until you start thinking or saying them to yourself automatically, the same way you used to say negative things.

Begin by choosing a topic or area in your life that you'd like to improve, most likely the area of your willpower project: health, energy levels, diet, exercise, promptness, self-confidence, or whatever area you'd like to focus on.

Now make a list of good things to tell yourself about your results. Tell yourself how happy and confident you feel. Tell yourself how much you enjoy pursuing your goals, how easy it is for you, how rewarding. You can expand your list to include any other good thing you'd like to tell yourself about your behavior or your life. Say more, rather than less.

You can use these affirmations in a number of ways:

- Choose two or three as your "thought for today" and repeat them to yourself as you get dressed in the morning, or drive to work, or during the day, or before you fall asleep at night. Say them instead of saying something nasty to yourself.
- Use technology to multiply your effectiveness: record your own tape cassette and play it to yourself once or twice a day. It's easy and phenomenally effective; never mind what the voice on the tape sounds like. Just read through your whole list of affirmations, pausing for two or three seconds between each thought. Say each affirmation with as much conviction as you can muster. Repeat the list until you've filled the tape.

Play the tape daily. After a few days or weeks, the affirmations will be nicely embedded in your thoughts. You can call on them quite easily.

THE LITTLE THEATER OF REALITY

Experiencing the good feelings associated with your positive affirmation is most easily done by using one of the most potent discoveries of modern science: visualization.

Visualization is simply linking your intention with your imagination. It's play acting: a full dress rehearsal of your future experience held in the present moment, with all the bells and whistles, sights, sounds, smells, and sensations of the real thing flowing through the theater of your mind.

You used to visualize all the time. Children visualize naturally. Do you remember how vivid and "real" the cowboys and Indians, the Cinderella coach, and the King of the Mountain were when you played games? Do you recall how engrossed you could become in something that you plainly knew was imaginary? That's visualization: not just "seeing" but *experiencing* the chosen event. You were *there*. Your muscles and heart rate and hormones responded just exactly as though you were really lifting off into space, or conquering the giant.

Those childhood visualizations, in many cases, have actually formed the internal positive affirmations for many, many successful people. Did you ever notice how many fabulously successful people say in an interview: "Ever since I was a child, I had dreamed of . . ." Or "I used to go home and pretend that I was . . ."? And since in their childhood visualizations, they really *were* rich and famous, or successful and loved by millions, today they actually are.

* * *

Willpower Lying Down

Physiologists have long known that when you imagine something quite vividly the muscles and nerves of your body respond to the imagined event in exactly the same way as they would if you were really experiencing the event physically. The nerves fire and the hormones flow in exactly the same way. There is no difference, physically, between reality and imagination.

This body-programming effect of visualization allows you to strengthen your willpower with very little physical effort. It's like willpower lying down, and in fact it works better if you're sitting or lying comfortably, your muscles and breathing relaxed and easy.

What you've already learned about entering the present moment is directly applicable to visualization and affirmation. All you need to add is this:

Inner Willpower Experience No. 16: Powerplay Visualization

Choose a time and place for your visualization where you can close your eyes undisturbed for a few moments. You may be seated or lying down.

Once you have entered the present moment, simply close your eyes and begin to play. Suspend all the rules of time and space, of what's real and what isn't and just have fun.

In your imagination, see yourself at the conclusion of your willpower project. See yourself happy, confident, relaxed, healthy, and in possession of whatever else you'd like to have or be.

If a visual image doesn't come immediately to mind, that's okay. Imagine the sounds, smells, colors, feelings, or any other sensations or symbols that feel right to you.

* * *

Now playfully begin to make this image or idea big, big, *big*, and even *bigger* until it is larger than the whole room, larger than the universe.

Make the colors brighter, the sounds louder, the smells richer. Allow the whole experience to become larger and larger.

Allow yourself to *be* it, bigger and bigger, more and more. Feel it. Envelop yourself in it. Step into it. Do it. Enjoy it.

You need only spend a few moments here. It isn't the amount of time or the number of repetitions that matter, but the intensity of your experience. Don't worry whether it's going to "work" or not. It will. Just have a good time, and go on with your day. The visualization will begin to work on its own, supporting and encouraging your best behavior.

16
Believing in Yourself

Belief—letting your affirmations become real to you—is the foundation of the good experiences that come from your affirmations.

Belief is what you get when your mind, emotions, and physical self are at one. When you attain this kind of integration and wholeness of self in a positive way, it is the mark of true inner willpower.

The Power of Belief

Because you believe, you achieve. With belief, there is no longer any internal conflict to drain your energies away from your actions. The inner belief comes first, and the appropriate external experience follows.

So if you say: "I can't believe that affirmation really works because my life never works out that way," you're really using a belief to propel an external result. How? Examine the above statement in the light of what you've learned about affirmation. Try this: change the words "cannot" and "never" to "will not." You get:

I will not believe that affirmation really
works because my life will not work out that way.

Are you hearing what your brain is actually hearing of the meaning of that statement? This is a very precise instruction to your mind, telling it to negate any effects of positive thinking. There's a belief—a will, an intent, a purpose—lying underneath the statement that is closing you off from results: a belief and a willing that you "will not believe." "But none of this ever works for me!" is a negative affirmation behind which you've unwittingly put your total imaginative commitment. You believe it as though it were true. So it becomes true, for you.

YOU'VE GOT TO BELIEVE IT TO SEE IT

You have experiences because of your beliefs. You don't have beliefs because of your experiences. This may seem contrary to all that you've ever learned about life.

Let's put aside those "I believe that fire is hot because I know darn well I burned my hand when I was two years old" type of belief-experiences. And look instead at belief as it is expressed in your more subjective opinions about life, people, yourself, and The Way It Is. Let's look at attitudes: those beliefs and opinions that might reasonably vary from person to person. It isn't necessary for you to revise your entire perception of reality in order to benefit from the changed experience that follows from some improved beliefs.

Did you ever notice how some of your unmarried friends seem to end up dating the same type of person over and over again? If you watch from a benign distance, their tales of romantic woe—or bliss—begin to assume a reliable familiarity over time, beginning or ending on the same repeated note. Your friend really believes that that's what women—or men—are all about. And if you're the recipient of their confidences you might, as someone older and wiser, someday suggest to them that "Gee, no wonder women treat you so badly! You expect them to leave you in the lurch, so you aren't even interested in a woman unless you can sense that she's trouble. . . ." It becomes very easy for us to solve our friend's problem: change his attitude, his expectations, his beliefs.

If we were truly offering compassionate advice to our romantically woebegone friend, we might say that he should not just change his attitudes about women, but change his attitudes toward himself, toward what he thinks he *deserves* in a relationship. It's good advice, but what you're really saying, in very practical terms, is: change your beliefs, and your experience will also change. It's very easy to see how negative beliefs can hinder other people.

But when it comes to changing our own beliefs, there's a problem: we believe them. We really, really think that they are true facts. You can choose to change your attitudes toward life fairly easily, once you become aware of them, but first you need that awareness.

Your beliefs can easily become invisible to you simply because they are so familiar that you stop seeing them. Think for a moment of the face of your oldest and dearest friend or of your spouse's face. Now: describe their nose. What does their nose really look like? Their nose is something you've looked at countless times, and yet, when you get right down to it, how much have you really seen of something that's literally as plain as that on their face? Beliefs, too, can become invisible when you take them for granted.

Here's a simple paper and pencil method for discovering outdated or hindering beliefs that may be holding you back from progress on your inner willpower project.

Inner Willpower Experience No. 17: The Facts of Life

Settle in with a paper and pencil, and choose a topic from this list:

* * *

What it's really like to be a man (or woman) today
What the company I work for is really like
What successful people are really like
What I'm really like
What losing weight is really all about
Why I can't get anything done
Why I can't quit smoking

Or choose a similar topic that you feel strongly about.

You're simply going to jot down some of the hard facts—the realities—about any of these topics. Nothing very subjective, just those things that are really, really true about the situation.

List the difficulties, the negatives, and the reasons why the situation is the way that it is. Let them reflect your best judgment, your cumulative experience with this topic. Let yourself express your real feelings for a few minutes.

Let your pencil flow. Perhaps there are some broader issues here, some reasons not strictly related, but somehow included. Just jot them down.

Adrienne, an assistant manager in a large hotel, chose to write about her work. Her list included things like:

The owners are foreign; they won't promote the locals to senior management.
No one ever takes me seriously.
I'm too short, and too young.
I haven't got enough education.
Women can't get ahead anyway.
If I get a promotion, my husband will be jealous.

Complete your own list of life's realities, Just go ahead and say them.

When you've finished your list, read down through it and add any other thoughts that occur to you.

THE FACTS OF BELIEF

Staring at you from that sheet of paper is actually a list of your beliefs! Every single thing you've written down here is a firmly held belief, disguised as a real true fact. A belief. Everything here is negotiable: a belief which you can choose to drop or modify. Seems incredible, doesn't it? Especially when your first reaction might be to defend the truth and reality of each of the statements. That's just exactly the point: you really do believe them.

This does not mean that everything you understand about life is false. This exercise demonstrates how invisible and yet prominent beliefs can be, and how firmly rooted they can become in your map of the world.

Read your list again. Some of these beliefs may appear to be quite indisputable facts. Let them be for now. But if you keep examining your list, you may begin to see that one or two ideas are tinged with an underlying attitude that may be defeatist or hostile or pessimistic. These "facts" hold your storehouse of negative feelings, a network of beliefs, perhaps, that you aren't good enough, or worthy enough to do well at something. And feelings, you will recall, are what link your thoughts to your physical reality.

THE BELIEF BEHIND THE BELIEF

At the root of negative or pessimistic beliefs is the feeling that you don't really deserve anything good, or any better than you have.

These fears and negative beliefs are not necessarily deeply buried and don't require years of psychoanalysis to root out. They are quite accessible to you. But because they are so familiar, and are taken for granted as "the way it really is," you've probably never bothered to really look at them.

You may want to jot down some other lists of the facts of life in an area that you feel you are being held back. And if you've ever wondered why positive affirmation "doesn't work" for you, you may find yourself saying "No wonder!" when you become aware of some of the other ideas and feelings you've been carrying around.

You may even discover specific areas where you've been at war with yourself, wanting, for instance, financial success but believing that "rich people aren't nice" or "poverty is more spiritual." Naturally, you could never really be committed to becoming a rich person if you believe the rich aren't nice people. Or you might want to lose weight but believe that "if I were thin I'd have to compete sexually" and find that distasteful. Or think that "as long as I'm sober I can't have any fun."

Dumping Useless Beliefs

Awareness, in and of itself, is a powerful dissolver of negativity. You can simply choose to release your negative beliefs, even if you are not specifically aware of what each of them are. It isn't necessary to understand every specific belief you may have in order to drop them.

You can use this Dumpster visualization whenever you'd like to drop old, unnecessary, negative beliefs. It has a wonderfully cleansing effect on the body as well as the emotions.

Inner Willpower Experience No. 18: The Dumpster

Close your eyes and enter the present moment by taking several long, deep, slow breaths. Make yourself comfortable. Take your time.

Become aware of your body. Feel what's happening inside your body, inside your breath.

When you are relaxed and comfortable, pretend that you are seated in front of a huge, empty, smelly garbage can. It is open, waiting to be filled. See its shape, its color, its vast size. Let your nose curl up at the faint smell.

Now begin to imagine that somewhere inside of you there's a lot of old, outmoded, unnecessary, unwanted, or irrelevant ideas and feelings. Garbage. You may sense shapes, or colors, or sizes. It may be simply a feeling, a sense. Just follow your instincts about anything that may be negative and unwanted, and about how it seems to you. It doesn't have to be specific.

Let the wisdom of your body and your inner self determine what you no longer need, what outmoded beliefs are holding you back, and what's no longer helpful to you. Allow your inner self to sort through every cell in your body, every atom, and to identify the garbage, the negativity, the depression. Simply allow this old junk to come free, whatever it may be.

Begin to pour this unwanted material into the garbage can. Just sense it streaming out of your body, out of all your cells, out of your breath, out of your pores, toward the garbage can which eagerly absorbs it.

Let the negative material continue to flow out. Add the worn out ideas, relationships, expectations, and thoughts, all the bad experiences and negative feelings. Add anything else you can't name but want to get rid of. Just let it go. Sense it streaming away from you. Simply observe it leaving your body. It no longer has anything to do with you. Just let it go.

Make the garbage can bigger and bigger; let it hold more and more. Continue as long as you'd like. Let go of everything you don't need. Take your time.

When the flow of garbage has finished, begin to imagine a celestial shower of brilliant, sparkling light surrounding you. Allow it to rinse down through your body, washing away the last bits of crud from your cells.

Let this liquid light cleanse away every lingering trace of old dirt. Let it wash through you like a crystalline tropical shower. Let go. Let yourself be made clean and true and fresh. Let it rinse away everything. Sparkle inside.

When you're ready, look at the garbage can in front of you, now filled with garbage. Put the lid on it firmly. Give it a loving, thankful pat and let go of the garbage can.

As you release the garbage can, see it begin to recede into the distance. See it speeding away from you, becoming smaller and smaller. Watch it go farther and farther away into the distance until it becomes a tiny dot and heads right into the flaming sun, where it is instantly vaporized. The garbage is no more. It is gone. You are free.

Take a deep, slow breath now and feel the changes in your body. Feel the fresh space you've created, and the sense of internal freedom you now have. Feel the energy of your body, the lightness, and the peace.

Sense or imagine the celestial light that still surrounds your body. Allow it to become brighter and clearer to your mind's eye. Let it become warmer and more secure, gentler and more protective.

Breathe in this kindly light. Let it soothe and restore all the cells in your body. Breathe gently, feeling more and more comfortable. Let the goodness and serenity of the light permeate you, healing all the tiny cracks and misunderstandings and leftover rough spots of your entire being. Feel it soothing everything into place, into harmony.

* * *

Feel how this light is filling you with goodness, with security and harmony. Breathe it in. Let it flow through you. Allow yourself to become stronger and stronger within this light.

Feel, now, that you really *are* the goodness, and the serenity, and the harmony. Acknowledge that this is truly you as you really are now: secure, strong, and good.

Feel how quiet your body is now: how safe, how harmonious, how pure it feels.

Affirm to yourself: I am good. I am worthwhile. I can choose to do good things for myself. I have perfect inner willpower. I am free. Feel the truth of these affirmations as they sink deeply and peacefully into the core of your being.

You can use The Dumpster visualization any time to remove negativity and unwanted emotional debris from your life. You can use it to affirm any new beliefs about yourself, your health, or your well-being that will enhance your life.

17

Beyond Willpower: Greater Help and Higher Resources

So what now, of your hopes and dreams?

What becomes of those things you wanted the inner willpower to accomplish? Where, finally, will the energy come from to sustain you on your journey toward your goals?

Now you have the tools. You've been shown the skills necessary to get in touch with your willpower. And you've made the essential connection to your inner life, to the source of your energy and strength.

But you don't have to "create" the energy of your inner willpower. You never did. You merely have to access it—tap into it—using the inner willpower skills you've learned here.

The Greater Energy

The energy, in fact, doesn't come from you at all. It never did. Yes, it is yours. And it is intimate and personal and uniquely designed to meet your needs. But it is not something you are creating when you practice the skills of being in the present moment.

It's better than that.

The energy that forms your inner willpower is an inexhaustible resource. It's in infinite supply, always ready, always fresh, always potent, always near at hand. You need only connect with it.

This energy is known by many names, in many languages, throughout every tradition and civilization. It is always the same, and yet takes many exquisite forms, shaped by the perceptions and needs of the individual, and of the time and place.

But always, it is at the center, at the core of life itself. It has been called the Great Spirit, Our Father, Mother Nature, the Force, the One, the Truth, the Sacred, All That Is, and God Itself.

Are you surprised that something so grand and far away can actually be so near and so familiar? So reassuring and secure and comfortable, so like your own truest self? But it is. Whenever you connect with your inner willpower, you have connected with this, with the great life force itself.

My purpose here is not to suggest to you how you ought to feel about these things, but to point out ways that you can continue to develop and strengthen the inner willpower that is one of the gifts of this extraordinary source. Whatever else you may wish to make of your access to the infinite is your personal privilege.

Nevertheless, this universal energy source is constantly available whenever you choose to align your inner circuits with it. Learning inner willpower is primarily a question of becoming more skilled at aligning yourself with this flow. After you've made the essential connection, the energy itself will act for you.

Group Power Is Stronger Than Willpower

But how do you stay in tune with the energy of inner willpower over the long haul? And where can you find support while you are building the successes and strong, secure disciplines that form the basis of your true commitment to your goals and to your best self?

There is another secret to inner willpower: that group power is stronger than willpower. Yes, it's true; you don't need to do this alone. A group of people with goals similar to your own can provide encouragement, support, and real energy for your progress. They can carry you along when you're down by providing you with the benefits of access to good energy on days when your own circuits feel depleted.

One of the best ways to make rapid progress on any program of personal development is to link up with a group of like-minded people, whether by joining a fitness club or diet workshop, church or community organization, or Alcoholics Anonymous, NarcAnon, or any of the myriad special-interest support groups available to you. A directory of support group clearing-houses is listed in Appendix B.

Especially if you are dealing with a true addiction beyond the scope of this book—to drugs, alcohol, other substances, or personal abuse—*you must have outside help* to overcome your addiction. Group support is the only method that's been shown to produce consistently good results with these immense personal challenges.

Yes, you need inner willpower to overcome your addiction. You've already made a big start. But with addiction everything you've learned here must be directed toward one simple project: getting yourself into treatment, making that phone call or going to that group meeting, getting yourself on the road to recovery. And everything you've learned here can be put to good use during your recovery and beyond. You've already started; you only need to take the next simple step. You can do it; I know you can.

Why is group energy so much stronger than your own? Because energy goes to energy. It's another of nature's universal laws that energy attracts similar energy—you might call it the Law of Coherence—and that more energy attracts more energy. That is, when two people have united toward a common goal, the circuit they create together attracts more than twice as much energy as each person could alone. Affiliating with a group that has goals similar to your own links you up with a powerhouse of positive energy. It has a real, measurable effect on your progress. You can actually do more acting together than you could each do individually.

That similar energy goes to similar energy is a fact that has some other interesting aspects. It is why "The rich get richer and the poor get poorer," and "What you do comes back to you," among other things. You get more of whatever you have. That's just the way that the life energy works.

In case these other aspects are creating some distracting thoughts—about forever attracting a geometric increase in your household bills or personal weaknesses, because that's what you seem to have the most of right now—you might want to refer back to the previous chapters on positive affirmations and beliefs. Essentially, you'll get more of whatever you *believe* that you have.

Life is as you see it; your attitude toward your life has an incredible influence on what comes to you. It's why your grandmother used to tell you to count your blessings: you get more of whatever you focus on. Hence the emphasis in this book on focusing on your positive traits, accomplishments, and strengths. That's where to place your energy, and that's what you'll attract more of.

Accessing group energy isn't purely a matter of taking something from the group, however. Although a group can certainly give you boundless amounts of support, encouragement, and everything you need to continue onward, nature's laws of natural energy also show that you can connect with group energy in its most beneficial form by giving back to your group, as well. Giving of your time, your experience, your love, and your own good energy. When you complete the circuit by giving, the energy flows through you powerfully and without hindrance.

You may at first feel that you have nothing to give to a support group that's worthwhile. You may feel that you can only take from the group. That's not true, and will eventually change if you stay with it. You actually have a tremendous wealth of personal experience in dealing with your own life, experience that can lend valuable advice and encouragement to others facing similar situations.

You have learned something worthwhile in your life that can help others, and you may not even realize it until you see someone else who is facing the thing that you are facing, and you see that your understanding can help ease the other person's pain. It's a tangible gift that you give at those times, simply by being there, simply by listening with quiet empathy and compassion. Oh yes, you have a great deal to give to a group.

What About Imposing Your Will?

Now that you've become acquainted with inner willpower, it's time to raise a few final questions. What, for instance, about imposing your will on others?

I hadn't seen Margaret in several months, when we met at a conference. She was visibly trimmer, and her skin and eyes glowed with new vitality. She was clearly pleased with her emerging lifestyle.

"It's great!" she said. "I haven't felt this good in ages."

She paused. "But now what do I do about my family's food? Bill's just not interested in changing his eating habits—and he needs it more than I do!"

"I know it's the right thing to do. But you should hear the complaining around the dinner table. . . ."

I commiserated. When we've found happiness for ourselves, we naturally want to share it with those closest to us. We hope to spare them some of the pain of their own journey in life.

But sometimes love demands more than that of us. It demands acceptance of those whom we love, as well as of ourselves. Acceptance of their right to have a will of their own, with their own goals and priorities, with their own inner life, and even their own destiny.

Just as you have the right to make your own choices as an adult, so must you permit others to choose freely, in their own way, in their own time.

This does not mean that you cannot set a good, loving example, or make alternatives available. But you cannot violate another's will, even with the best of motives, even "for their own good." After all, how effective is it if someone tries to do that to you?

You must operate with goodwill and harmony, especially within your family or among your closest associates. You cannot contribute anything to your own inner harmony and balance if you sow discord around yourself.

Marriage, especially, is a kind of three-legged race. If you try to run too fast ahead of your partner, you will both stumble and fall.

Margaret nodded. "I guess I should be offering my family fruit sorbet desserts instead of lecturing about why they can't eat ice cream.

"Maybe Bill will come around, too" she added. "He does make jokes about how gorgeous I'm getting. . . ."

Margaret hesitated, with a canape poised in midbite. "There's something else: What do I do about these things? I mean, whenever I go to a party, there's usually someone who insists on pushing food on me.

"It almost seems like a battle of wills: mine versus theirs . . ."

The trick here is to avoid turning the issue into a direct confrontation. Your objective, after all, is to avoid eating the undesirable food or doing the undesirable thing, not to "win" a contest of wills.

Use a little verbal judo to sidestep the challenge, I suggested. Agree that yes, you'd love some, but maybe you'll have it in a few minutes or a little later? You can be fuzzy as to exactly when.

Your host or hostess has not been refused, you've appreciated their fine offering, so they haven't "lost." But somehow, in the tide of pleasant conversation and good company, you never quite get around to having any. So you've also won.

In more dire circumstances, you can avoid a direct refusal by again agreeing that yes, it would be wonderful, but also muttering something about unfortunately being wildly allergic . . . Or doctor's orders . . . Or this awful medication I have to take . . . Very few people will quibble with a refusal that seems to have nothing to do with the quality of their hospitality or your own personal taste.

Margaret grinned. I'd noticed something else about her: she'd eaten only one canape. Was this her new inner willpower at work?

She looked at her empty cocktail napkin with bemusement. "You know, I hadn't thought about that. But I'm just so much more aware of enjoying what I *do* eat, that somehow eating one is as good as eating a dozen used to be. . . ."

She plopped the napkin victoriously onto a passing tray. Her laughter was joyous.

"Next . . . I'm taking up mountain climbing!"

And so one day, may you.

Appendix A

SOME FURTHER PRESENT MOMENT EXPERIENCES TO TRY

Now that you have a better appreciation of the importance of being able to shift your awareness more fully into the here and now, you may want to experiment with a few other techniques for accomplishing this. Here are several that you can do any time, anywhere.

Each of these techniques will produce that relaxed state of "centeredness" and well-being that you most likely experienced with the Present Moment Exercise at the beginning of the book. You can make games for yourself out of these. Once you've gotten the knack, you can quickly bring yourself into the here and now throughout the day with just a few relaxed breaths and a moment's thought.

Try each of these as an experiment; you may find that one of them "clicks" quite naturally with your personal taste and temperament. You can practice it, or the basic breathing exercise, whenever you want to collect your energies for better willpower.

Remember, bringing yourself into the present moment is the basic skill for learning all other willpower skills. Come back and do any of these exercises—or the Present Moment Exercise on page 9—once or twice a day for the next few days, until the knack for slipping easily into the present moment begins to feel comfortable.

Begin each experience by reminding yourself of what you want to do, perhaps by saying to yourself: "Now I'm going to relax and experience the present moment, right here."

Basic Power Breathing

You may find it useful right now to think back to some previous time that you felt truly relaxed and centered—perhaps to when you were doing the Present Moment Exercise, or to a special time or place. See the surroundings in your mind's eye.

Allow your body to "remember" that experience by feeling some of the relaxed sensations, as though you were in that special time and place right now. Let the feeling wash right over you. If nothing comes to mind, or you don't feel anything in particular, that's okay. It will get easier with practice. Just carry on with this "game."

This next part, though, is the crucial step for every experience: become aware of your breathing.

Just become aware: observe your breath flowing in, and out. Don't change anything; don't deliberately begin breathing faster or slower. Just let your body respond naturally. Whether you're sitting in your car or walking down the street or making dinner, just notice that you *are* breathing, and *how* you are breathing. You may keep your eyes open, unless it is convenient for you to close them for a few moments to shut out distractions.

Breathe normally and follow the breath with your full attention. In. And out. Follow each breath. Feel it flow in and out of your nostrils. Observe it flowing in and out of your body. Feel your chest and your belly moving quietly in and out. Notice the flow of life-giving air.

Continue observing your breath until it seems to be the most important element in your life at this moment. Don't rush. There's nothing to be or do except breathe. When you are fully aware of your breathing and feeling comfortable with it, simply notice how your body feels right now.

Now let go of any leftover tension you've been hanging onto in your hands, in your arms, shoulders or neck. Feel it all draining out the soles of your feet like a liquid, feel as though each inward breath were a fresh, crystalline shower that could flow right through your inner being, washing away all the staleness, all the fatigue. Let the tensions flow out for as long as you need to; there's no hurry.

The Body Energy Inventory

After you've become aware of your breathing using Basic Power Breathing, simply become aware of your body as you breathe.

Feel your chest and belly rise and fall to the rhythm of your breathing. Become aware of your arms and legs. Simply "sit" inside your body and feel how the bones and muscles are arranged in space.

Feel how your body feels. What's tight? What's loose? What's warm or cool? Feel how your feet are contacting the ground. Where are your hands? Feel them. What's inside your body? Any aches or tensions or discomfort? Simply notice them, without changing anything.

Simply feel the presence of your body right now. Focus your attention on it, here in this place, right now. There isn't anything else to be or do. Simply be where your body is.

Observe any changes in the way you feel or in your body sensations or energy as a result of this experience.

* * *

Say to yourself: "This is the present moment. I am fully here, in my body, right now."

The Hearing Game

Once you've become focused on your breath and feel relaxed and comfortable, simply open your ears and, without trying to understand everything or decide what it is, begin to listen to all the ordinary sounds around you. Listen to all the sounds at once, without trying to sort anything out or block anything. Merely let your ears relax and "reach" as far in all directions as they wish.

Sit and listen to the levels of sound, and the differences coming from different directions. You'll hear distant traffic, perhaps, or the hum of air conditioners, voices, TVs, or general buzzing, whirring, and whooshing coming from all directions.

You may be quite surprised at how much sound you can suddenly hear from the quiet place where you are sitting now.

This is an ideal focusing exercise to try while you are walking down a street, perhaps, or driving in your car. Listen to your own footsteps, or those of others as they approach and pass you. Listen for the changing echoes as you walk by buildings or doorways. What can you learn about the size and shape of the space you are in from its sounds?

Immerse yourself totally in the sea of sound surrounding you. Say to yourself: "All of this is the present moment, here and now."

* * *

The Ocean of Air

This variation is the most subtle, but once you get the hang of it, will improve the perceptive abilities of all your senses very quickly, as well as move you promptly and fully into the present moment.

Once you've focused on your breathing, remind yourself that at sea level there's about fourteen pounds per square inch of air pressure pressing gently against everything. The air around you, and the air that you breathe, actually has weight and substance. It flows like a magical, luminescent liquid to fill all the space around you.

Simply become aware of the surface of your skin. See if you can feel, or imagine, the gently supportive presence of the air pressing tenderly against your skin. Become aware of the surface of your body. Is it smooth or rough? Warm or cool? Where does your body end and the air begin?

What can you feel about the air? What can you sense about its presence? Is it bright? Or dark? Heavy? Light? Still? Moving? What qualities does it have at this moment?

Take a deep, refreshing breath and say to yourself: "This ocean of air is the present moment. I am here, now."

Appendix B

FINDING A SUPPORT GROUP

This is a partial list of support group clearinghouses. They'll help you locate a support group that's right for you.

National Self-Help Clearinghouse
25 West 43rd Street—Room 620
New York, NY 10036
(212) 642-2944

California Self-Help Center
2327 Franz Hall
405 Hilgard Avenue
Los Angeles, CA 90024–1563
(213) 825-1799

Illinois Self-Help Center
1600 Dodge Avenue, Suite S-122
Evanston, IL 60201
(708) 328-0470 or (312) 876-0010

Massachusetts Clearinghouse of Mutual Help Groups
Skinner Hall—Room 113
University of Massachusetts
Amherst, MA 01003
(413) 545-2313

First Call for Help
United Way of St. Paul Area
166 East 4th Street, Suite 310
St. Paul, MN 55101–1448
(612) 224-1133

Self-Help Clearinghouse of Greater Washington
7630 Little River Turnpike, Suite 206
Annandale, VA 22003
(703) 642-0800

Or contact your local church, school district, or United Way.

Appendix C

DEEPENING YOUR EXPERIENCE

If you'd like to explore further this book's approach to inner willpower, send for the complimentary catalog of programs, seminars, and workshops offered exclusively by:

Kripalu Center for Yoga and Health
Box 793
Lenox, MA 01240
(413) 637-3280

INDEX